JOHN R. TYSON

PRAYING WITH THE WESLEYS

FOUNDATIONS OF METHODIST SPIRITUALITY

Praying with the Wesleys: Foundations of Methodist Spirituality

The General Board of Higher Education and Ministry leads and serves The United Methodist Church in the recruitment, preparation, nurture, education, and support of Christian leaders—lay and clergy—for the work of making disciples of Jesus Christ for the transformation of the world. The General Board of Higher Education and Ministry of The United Methodist Church serves as an advocate for the intellectual life of the church. The Board's mission embodies the Wesleyan tradition of commitment to the education of laypersons and ordained persons by providing access to higher education for all persons.

Wesley's Foundery Books is an imprint of the General Board of Higher Education and Ministry, The United Methodist Church, and named for the abandoned foundery that early followers of John Wesley transformed into a ministry, which became the cradle of London's Methodist movement.

Praying with the Wesleys: Foundations of Methodist Spirituality

All web addresses were correct and operational at the time of publication.

GBHEM Publishing is an affiliate member of the Association of University Presses.

ISBN 978-1-945935-54-1

Manufactured in the United States of America

HIGHER EDUCATION & MINISTRY
General Board of Higher Education and Ministry
THE UNITED METHODIST CHURCH

Contents

Acknowledgments

Just as it "takes a village to raise a child," it takes a community to birth, nurture, and grow a spiritual tradition. Our Wesleyan spirituality was a child with many parents, several of whom we will listen to in the current volume. In a similar way this volume was nurtured and shaped by the prayers, questions, and conversations I've had with the people called Methodists— largely in the Upper New York Annual Conference—who participated and shared so freely in the various "teach-ins," retreats, and lecture series I hosted on this topic. I offer them my thanks, and I dedicate this small offering of gratitude to them.

I am also grateful to Dr. Kathy Armistead, publisher, General Board of Higher Education and Ministry, The United Methodist Church. Her support, direction, and insight on this project was invaluable. And, finally, I thank you, dear reader, for picking up this little book. It is my sincere hope and prayer that it brings blessing to your life.

Introduction

Among the Methodists, stories about Susanna, John, and Charles Wesley abound. In our mind's eye we can see Susanna bustling about the kitchen of the Epworth manse, shaping the young lives of her nine children. We might even imagine John Wesley, traveling preacher and evangelical centaur—half man, half horse—living out his life trying to "spread scriptural holiness" across the land. We assign Charles a more dreamy, mystical role as the poet laureate of the movement and creative force behind the more than 9,000 hymns that became the soundtrack for the Wesleyan revival. Each of these caricatures is accurate, to some degree, but they are also pretty much useless to us, as we try to tap into the spiritual energy that empowered their lives and gave birth to Methodist tradition—of which more than 80.5 million of us are descendants and heirs.

Our past acts as a distant mirror in which we can catch glimpses of our truest selves. Our histories offer a context for understanding who we were, who we are, and who we might be able to become. We live in times that beg for a such a clear assessment, and reassessment, both in terms of who we are as practicing Christians and as "the people called Methodists." We need to ask once again from whence have we come, in order to have some clear sense of where we could or should be headed and to help us mark out a new path. Indeed, it seems that our current challenges loom so very large that perhaps we should pray like Elisha (2 Ki. 2:9) of old for a double portion of the Spirit that was in our founders and overflowed to change the world. Would that we could we drink deeply of the Spirit!

While there are resources available to help us pray, surprisingly little has been done to examine what was and is most characteristic about Wesleyan spirituality and how it can be better appropriated for our own use in these current, challenging times. This is precisely the task that I hope to begin in this volume. We will look at the roots, impact, and trajectories of early Methodist spirituality, as it was epitomized by Susanna, John, and Charles Wesley, hoping—indeed, praying—that this exercise will help us chart a new course for ourselves and for the community of faith, described by Charles Wesley as "the old ship," as we sail through the rough water of these times.

Prayer, in its various forms, clearly predominates the enterprise of being heirs of Susanna, John, and Charles Wesley. Perhaps this point is so obvious that it is too obvious to mention. We know that they lived prayerful lives. For example, the new "critical edition" of John Wesley's works registers 5,418 "hits" on a word search for "prayer"; this collection includes none of Susanna's writings and offers only a very small sampling of Charles's voluminous corpus of hymns. Stories of John Wesley's prayer life abound—rising at 4:00 a.m., writing rules and drafting holy resolutions without end, dividing his day into fifteen-minute segments for prayer, reflection, and personal accountability. This picture is both astonishing and useless to us, unless we find a way to tap into the spiritual energy and transformative impact that John Wesley (and indeed Susanna and Charles) found in prayer.

In what follows, we will attempt to look at the formative development of Wesleyan spirituality from its earliest roots with the fervent hope that observing some of its inner dynamics will enable us to drink in (perhaps) a "double portion" of the spirit that was in Susanna, John, and Charles. What we learn from them will certainly help carry us forward through our own difficult days.

Wesleyan spirituality is a composite work—like a mosaic made of variegated stones—of resources drawn from "the primitive church," Anglicanism, Puritanism, and Moravianism. It is also clear that these various elements were creatively shaped and enhanced by the lives, personalities, and life challenges of our first founders. In the following work you will encounter nine short chapters of historical assessment, reassessment, and spiritual reflection. The reader will find five small collections of representative prayers and hymns (Appendices A–E) from Susanna, John, and Charles Wesley, which illustrate and, hopefully, will help instill in us their vibrant spirituality and prayerful vision of life.

One

Roots of a Prayerful Life

In one of his mid-career letters to his younger brother Charles, John Wesley reminded both of them of their own illustrious heritage in Christian ministry: "So far as I can learn, such a thing has scarce been for these thousand years before, as a son, father, grandfather . . . preaching the gospel, nay and the genuine gospel, in a line."[1] This "line" reached back through both their father Samuel and mother Susanna Annesley Wesley to their grandfathers. While this heritage may have carried weight in terms of the vocational choices of at least two of Samuel and Susanna's sons (John and Charles), it also shaped the spiritual lives of all nine of the Wesley children. In the first twenty-five years of marriage Susanna and Samuel had nineteen children, only ten of whom survived infancy, and their parents sought to "train up" each one of them "in the way he [or she] should go."

Neither Samuel nor Susanna's fathers supported the Church of England. They were Puritans who sought to reform the Anglican communion by reshaping it according to the religious and theological proclivities of a staunch continental Calvinism. This meant that the Puritans intended to "purify" the Church of England of its Roman Catholic trappings by enforcing a Calvinist view on Christian worship and salvation. They sought to purge the Church of all the vestiges of the *via media* ("middle way") compromise between Protestantism and Catholicism that was worked out a

1   John Telford, ed., *The Letters of the Rev. John Wesley, A.M.* in 7 vol. (London: Epworth Press, 1931), Vol. V, 76.

century before in the Elizabethan Settlement. The employment of colorful vestments, processions and recessions, visual Christianity, formal liturgies, kneeling for prayer, the use of incense, making the sign of the cross, episcopal church government, and—perhaps most notably—the use of the *Book of Common Prayer* as the guide for personal and corporate worship were all eschewed by the Puritans. These very same trappings were removed from Church life during the decade they dominated both Church and State in England (circa 1649–60).

Following a decade of religious and political turmoil, the monarchy was restored in May 1660. The so-called "Caroline Divines," who ascended to religious leadership following the fall and ouster of the Puritans, worked to reverse all their religious and spiritual changes. They hated the Puritans' bare style of worship as well as their narrow, predestinarian understanding of God's acceptance. Where the Puritans had been staunch Calvinists, who insisted that God's unconditional election and absolute predestination determined the destiny of both the saved and damned, their successors were Arminians, who believed that Christ died for all people and God's grace and acceptance was open and readily accessible to all. Where the Puritans sought to purge the Church of "popish" forms of government and "Romish" styles of worship, the pastors and theologians of the Restoration era sought a return to the Anglican "middle way," which embraced Catholic forms of worship as well as Protestant theology.

The Wesley family originally hailed from the West of England and were known as the "Westleys." The great-grandfather of John and Charles, Bartholomew Westley (1596–1680), was pastor at Allington, near Bridgeport, during this period of profound religious turmoil. He was a staunch Puritan, who upon the restoration of the monarchy refused to use the Anglican *Book of Common Prayer* either publicly or privately. He was, therefore, brought up on charges in 1661, removed from his parish, and separated from the Church in 1662 under the *Act of Uniformity*, which required all English clergy to embrace the *Book of Common Prayer*. He was in this sense a conscientious objector—or to use the language of the time—a "dissenter" and "nonconformist." Bartholomew's eldest son, John Westley (1636–78)—the grandfather of John and Charles—was also a Puritan pastor who was deprived of his living and stood apart from the Anglican establishment. Born in the same year that the monarchy and Church of

England were restored in England, Westley's son, Samuel Wesley (1662–1735), the father of John and Charles, was also raised and educated in the same Puritan tradition.

Dr. Samuel Annesley (1620–96), Susanna Wesley's father, was a prominent theologian and church leader among the Puritans. He rose to prominence during the Puritan regime and was called to pastor a church in St. Giles, Cripplegate, London. He, too, was forced to leave the Church of England during the Restoration, and thereby established a dissenting community in a meeting house on Bishopsgate Street, London. Annesley was a well published theologian and popular preacher whose congregation soon grew to more than 800. It also became a focal point for religious dissent in London; he was known as "the St. Paul of the Nonconformists."[2] Dr. Annesley was lovingly eulogized in verse by one of his famous parishioners, the novelist Daniel Defoe. His precocious twenty-fifth daughter Susanna (1669–1742)—the mother of the founders of Methodism—was barred from formal education because of the social restrictions placed upon women in her day. Nevertheless, she compensated for her lack of formal education by reading every book in her illustrious father's library. She, too, was steeped in Puritan spirituality and communicated several aspects of it to her children. She would be known as "the mother of Methodism."

Ironically, both Samuel Wesley and Susanna Annesley left Puritanism to embrace the Church their parents rejected: the Church of England. They did so with great gusto and at significant cost in terms of financial and familial support. Samuel apparently had a dramatic change of ecclesiastical heart while reading the works of Bishop Tillotson as he studied at a Puritan academy (circa 1680). Cut off from school and family, young Sam "footed it" to Oxford with only forty-five shillings in his pocket and all his worldly possessions in a knapsack on his back. There he enrolled in Exeter College as a "servitor," where he maintained himself by acting as a servant to wealthier students, and by publishing epigrams, articles, and poems.[3]

---

2   John Newton, *Susanna Wesley and the Puritan Tradition* (London: Epworth Press, 1968), 19.

3   Luke Tyerman, *The Life and Times of the Rev. Samuel Wesley, M.A., Rector of Epworth, and Father of the Revs. John and Charles Wesley, the Founders of the Methodists*

Susanna's spiritual journey from Puritanism towards support for the Church of England has been described as a product of her growing relationship with Samuel "as love and theological accord ripened together."[4] Her own writings, however, suggest it was much more a product of her own theological explorations:

> Because I had been educated among the Dissenters, and there being something remarkable in my leaving them at so early an age, not being full thirteen, I had drawn up an accord of the controversy between them and the Established Church, as far as it had come to my knowledge; and then followed the reasons which had determined my judgment to the preference of the Church of England.[5]

When they married, in 1688, Susanna was nineteen or twenty, and Samuel was already well on his way to becoming a priest in the Church of England. By the time he was ordained in 1690, Samuel warmly embraced the emphasis on sacraments and liturgical style that was characteristic of "High Church" Anglicanism. Having made up her own mind about church style and affiliation five years before, Susanna was equally committed to the Church. Not surprisingly, like their father and mother, both John and Charles Wesley developed a deep attachment to the Church of England. "I am a Church-of-England man,"[6] John Wesley told his friend Henry Moore, and later in one of his sermons John explained: "I hold all the doctrines of the Church of England. I love her Liturgy. I approve of her plan of discipline, and only wish it could be put into execution." [7] Charles Wesley, for his part, spent a significant portion of his own ministry trying to keep the Methodists from separating from the Church of England.[8] It was in this sense, then,

(London: Simpkin, Marshall and Co., 1866), 79–82.

4   Newton, *Susanna Wesley*, 66.

5   Dr. John Whitehead, *The Life of Rev. John Wesley, M.A. . . . With Some Account of His Ancestors and Relations* (Boston: Jm. McLeish, 1844), 37.

6   Telford, ed., *Letters of JW*, Vol. VIII, 58, "Letter to Henry Moore, May 11, 1788."

7   Albert Outler, ed., *The Works of John Wesley: Sermons IV*, 115–51 (Nashville: Abingdon Press, 1987), 80, Sermon #121, "Prophets and Priests."

8   Cf. John R. Tyson, *Assist Me to Proclaim: The Life and Hymns of Charles Wesley* (Grand Rapids, MI: Eerdmans, 2007), 215–29.

that Garret Lloyd aptly described Charles as "a self-appointed guardian of the Church-Methodist gate."[9]

The Puritan spiritual instruction that both Samuel and Susanna received in their youth left an indelible and discernable spiritual imprint on them. In Samuel this could be seen, perhaps most clearly, in his ongoing concern for the development of the inner life. He was also deeply affected by a spiritual resurgence that shook Oxford University during his student days. His devotional reading in works like *The Whole Duty of Man* urged "the general duty preparatory of all the rest, [that is] consideration and care of their own souls."[10] Practical Christian concerns like spiritual disciplines, small groups, and preparation for receiving the Lord's Supper, which he met in the writings of Anthony Horneck (1641–97), impressed Samuel with the importance the personal cultivation of inner life alongside the liturgical forms and means of grace urged by the Anglican communion.[11]

John lovingly remembered his father's fusion of the inner and outer life as even being echoed in Samuel's dying words to him: "'The inward witness, son, the inward witness,' he said to me, 'that is the proof, the strongest proof, of Christianity.'"[12] And Susanna, who had been raised in "an outstanding example of a Puritan household where demanding educational standards accompanied disciplined devotional and moral teaching,"[13] implemented these very same practices in the education and nurture of

---

9   Gareth Lloyd, *Charles Wesley and the Struggle for Methodist Identity* (Oxford: Oxford University Press, 2007), 163.

10 H. Hammond, ed., *The Whole Duty of Man Laid Down in a Plain and Familiar Way [. .] for Several Occasions* (London: W. Norton, 1704), 3. First published anonymously in 1668, the book has been attributed to various authors, including most recently Richard Allestree. The premise of the work is based on Ecclesiastes 12:13 (KJV), which urges: "Let us hear the conclusion of the whole matter: Fear God, and keep his commandments: for this is the whole duty of man."

11 Born in Germany and educated at Lincoln College, Oxford, Rev. Anthony Horneck became a prominent pastor and preacher in the Church of England. Many of his sermons were published, and among his influential devotional works were: *The Great Law of Consideration [. .] Betwixt a Christian and His Own Conscience* (1683).

12 Frank Baker, ed., *The Works of John Wesley, Vol. 26, Letters II, 1740–1755* (Oxford: Clarendon Press, 1982), Letter to John Smith, March 22, 1748, 288.

13 Robert C. Monk, *John Wesley: His Puritan Heritage* (London: Epworth Press, 1966), 21.

her own children.[14] The family tree, religious heritage, and home life in the Epworth manse suggest that the co-founders of Methodism, John (1703–91) and Charles (1707–88) Wesley, imbibed and would continue to develop a spirituality that was a rich mixture of Anglican "means"—worship practices and prayer life—and Puritan religious "affections"—the cultivation of an inward life through spiritual disciplines.

14 Cf. Charles Wallace, ed., *Susanna Wesley: The Complete Writings* (Oxford: Oxford University Press, 1997), 367–76, "On Educating My Children."

Two

Train Up a Child

Samuel and Susanna Wesley believed and most emphatically followed the advice of Proverbs 22:6 that urged parents: "Train up a child in the way he should go: and when he is old, he will not depart from it." They employed a skillful division of labor to accomplish the task of raising nine faithful children, which they considered to be both a ministry and a holy duty. Susanna operated an impromptu primary school in her kitchen while Samuel taught the boys (and several of the talented girls) logic, Latin, Greek, church history, and theology in his study. Writing later in life, John recalled: "From a child I was taught to love and reverence the Scripture, the oracles of God; and, next to these, to esteem the primitive Fathers, the writers of the first three centuries. Next after the primitive church I esteemed our own, the Church of England."[1] Several of the children, including Samuel Jr., Hetty, John, and Charles, emulated their father's poetical muse. It was Susanna's duty to teach her ever-growing brood of children to read, write, and pray. Looking back from the distance of many years, however, John recalled

> having been strictly educated and carefully taught that I could only be saved by universal obedience, by keeping all the commandments of God, in the meaning of which I was diligently instructed. And those

1   Thomas Jackson, ed., *The Works of John Wesley, A.M.*, 14 vol., "Farther Thoughts on Separation from the Church," (1789), Vol. IX, 538.

instructions, so far as they respected outward duties and sins, I gladly received and often thought of. But all that was said to me of inward obedience or holiness I neither understood nor remembered.[2]

In a letter to her husband, who was away at a church conference, Susanna explained her approach to parenting as a spiritual ministry:

> Though I am not a man or a minister of the gospel and so cannot be employed in such a worthy employment at they were; yet, if my heart were sincerely devoted to God, and if I were inspired with a true zeal for his glory and did really desire the salvation of souls . . . I am resolved to begin with my own children.[3]

At this same juncture she described "her method" for shaping the spiritual life of her children:

> I take such a proportion of my time as I can best spare every night to discourse with each child by itself on something that relates to its principal concerns. On Monday I talk with Molly, on Tuesday with Hetty, Wednesday with Nancy, Thursday with Jacky, Friday with Patty, Saturday with Charles, and with Emily and Sukey together on Sunday.[4]

A vivid example of the impact of these spiritual conversations survived in John Wesley's recollections and understanding of his narrow escape from the flames when the Epworth Rectory caught fire and burned to the ground on August 24, 1709. Six-year-old "Jacky's" deliverance from the flames was given theological significance by his mother, who subsequently wrote an account of it.[5] And it was probably through those precious one-on-one conversations with her that John Wesley came to understand himself, in the phraseology of Zechariah 3:2, as "a brand plucked out of the burning"—providentially preserved by God for some great future work. The "brand plucked out of the burning" phraseology was also subsequently used by John to describe deliverance (his

---

2   W. Reginald Ward and Richard P. Heitzenrater, eds., *The Works of John Wesley: Vol. 18, Journals and Diaries I* (1735–1738) entry for May 24, 1738 (Nashville: Abingdon Press, 1988), 243.

3   Ward and Heitzenrater, "Letter to Samuel," dated August 4, 1704, *Works of JW*, 50.

4   Ward and Heitzenrater, "Letter to Samuel," 50.

5   See Susanna Wesley's description of the fire in Wallace, ed., *Susanna Wesley*, 65–66.

own and others) from future loss in perdition. Methodist preacher Henry Moore heard Wesley recount his childhood deliverance in this way,[6] and John himself considered the event important enough to mention it in the epitaph he wrote for himself (but did not need at that point) on November 26, 1753.[7]

In a letter to her Oxford don son, John (dated July 24, 1732), Susanna recalled:

> The children of this family were taught, as soon as they could speak, the Lord's Prayer, which they were made to say at rising and bedtime constantly; to which as they grew bigger, were added a short prayer for their parents, and some collects; a short catechism, and some portions of Scripture, as their memories could bear. . . . They were as soon taught to be still at family prayers, and to ask a blessing immediately after, which they used to do by signs, before they could kneel or speak.[8]

That Susanna nurtured her children's spiritual life out of the deep well of her own devotions is made clear by the recent discovery of fragments of her prayer journal, which carries reflective daily entries for morning, noon, and evening, on topics such as the examination of conscience, battling temptations, seeking the presence of God, and the use of spiritual disciplines and practices.[9] Nor is it surprising, given their division of spiritual labors, that the Wesley boys, when they were away at college, plied their mother with spiritual questions while they wrote their father about Christian doctrine.

The Wesley children's formal education also began at an early age in Susanna's little school in the kitchen. She explained,

> None of them were taught to read till five years old. . . . The way of teaching was this. The day before a child began to learn, the house was set in

---

6   Henry Moore, *The Life of John Wesley, A.M.* in 2 vol. (New York: 1826), Vol. I, 69.

7   Ward and Heitzenrater, eds., *Works of JW*, Vol. XX, *Journal and Diaries III* (1743–1754), 482. John Wesley wrote: "Here Lieth the body of John Wesley, a brand plucked out of the burning, who died of a consumption in the Fifty-first year of his age. Not leaving after his debts are paid, ten pounds behind him. Praying 'God be merciful to me,' an unprofitable servant!"

8   Cf. Wallace, ed., *Susanna Wesley*, 371.

9   Wallace, 215–362.

order, everyone's work appointed them, and a charge given that none should come into the room from nine to twelve, or from two till five; which . . . were our school hours. One day was allowed the child wherein to learn its letters. . . . As soon as they knew the letters they were put first to spell; and read one line, then a verse [from the Bible], never leaving till perfect in their lesson, were it shorter or longer. So one or other continued reading at school—time without any intermission, and before we left school each child read what he had learned that morning; and we parted in the afternoon, what they had learned that day.[10]

The children learned to read at various paces, but it is clear that they were reading the Bible beginning at the age of five, and other devotional readings, such as those from the *Book of Common Prayer,* soon followed.[11] These early devotional practices, as well as their participation in worship and sacraments of the Epworth Church, gave them a strong spiritual foundation that, in the case of many, withstood the tests of time and distress.[12]

After a brief initial pastorate in South Ormsby from 1694 to 1696, Samuel and Susanna Wesley and their growing family settled into the Anglican manse at Epworth. Samuel was already deeply in debt by 1700, as he explained to his bishop by letter: "I must own, I was ashamed . . . to confess that I was £300 in debt, when I have a living of which I have made £200 per annum"[13] The "gentile poverty" caused by their constant indebtedness caused the Wesleys' Puritan proclivities toward careful stewardship to merge with their real-world needs to develop a careful and simple (sometimes Spartan) lifestyle, which was emulated, with varying degrees of success, by their children. More to the point, it left both John and Charles Wesley with a keen sense of the sting of poverty, which moved them beyond empathy to action on behalf of the poor—both as

---

10 Wallace, 371.

11 Wallace, 371, regarding Samuel Jr.'s progress in reading Genesis, for example.

12 See Wallace, 425–79, for Susanna's written recollection of conversations she had with her daughter and subsequently used as a catechism with her other children. The spiritual struggles of John and Charles Wesley are fairly well known, but the same sort of resilience and spiritual strength also can be observed among their sisters. See, for example, Frederick E. Maser, *Seven Sisters in Search of Love: The Story of John Wesley's Sisters* (Rutland: Academy Books, 1988).

13 Telford, *Samuel Wesley,* 230.

college students and then as ministers.[14] But vital Christian stewardship extends beyond economic justice; because genuine Christian stewardship embraces all aspects of life as gifts from God, it infuses all of one's life with a deep sense of gratitude and carefulness. As John Wesley would later write in one of his sermons, "[Let the Christian] so account himself as a steward of the manifold gifts of God, let him see that all his thoughts, and words, and works, are agreeable to the post God has assigned him. It is no small thing to lay out *for* God all which you have received *from* God."[15]

This concern included the stewardship of one's time and talents and led to John's meticulously annotated diaries, which accounted for his time in specific segments—sometimes as small as fifteen-minute intervals;[16] it also encompassed matters such as the use of one's money,[17] natural resources,[18] and humanitarian issues such as social justice.[19] John's prayerful closing to his sermon "On Riches" voiced these sentiments:

> O Let your heart be whole with God! Seek your happiness in him and him alone. Beware that you cleave not to the dust! This *earth* is not your place. See that you use this world as not abusing it; *use* the world, and *enjoy* God. Sit as loose to all things here below as if you was a poor beggar.
>
> Be a good steward of the manifold gifts of God, that when you are called to give an account of your stewardship he may say, "Well done, good and faithful servant; enter thou into the joy of thy Lord."[20]

---

14 See, for example, Theodore W. Jennings, *Good News to the Poor: John Wesley's Evangelical Economic* (Nashville: Abingdon, 1990), and S. T. Kimbrough, *Radical Grace: Justice for the Poor and Marginalized—Charles Wesley's Views for the Twenty-First Century* (Eugene, OR: Cascade Books, 2013).

15 Vol. II, *Sermons 2*, #51, "The Good Steward," 298. Emphasis added.

16 See, for example, W. Reginald Ward and Richard P. Heitzenrater, eds., *The Works of John Wesley: Vol. 18, Journals and Diaries I* (1735–38) (Nashville: Abingdon Press, 1988), 312–574.

17 See, for example, John Wesley's sermons #50 "The Use of Money"; #87 "The Danger of Riches"; and #131 "The Danger of Increasing Riches."

18 See, for example, John Wesley's treatise, "Thoughts on the Present Scarcity of Provisions," in Thomas Jackson, ed., *Works of John Wesley, A.M.*, 14 vol. (London: Wesleyan Conference, 1872), Vol. XI, 53–59.

19 Jackson, ed., "Thoughts Upon Slavery," 59–80.

20 Outler, ed., *Vol III, Sermons 3*, #108, "On Riches," 528.

Alongside their profound recognition that all of human life was to be understood as lived out in the presence of God, and as a gift from God, stood a willingness to use self-reflection, to ascertain whether one was in fact ordering her or his inner and outer life in accordance with God's will and intentions for us. The Puritans called this spiritual exercise "the examination of conscience," and the Wesleys came by this discipline quite honestly; Susanna's illustrious father, Samuel Annesley published an important book on this topic.[21] The very first sermon in the collection, edited by Dr. Annesley, was also written by him. It was based on the scripture, "And herein do I exercise myself, to have always a conscience void of offence toward God, and toward men" (Acts. 24:16). Susanna's father titled his message with the provocative question: "How May We Be Universally Conscientious?"

As the sermon moved towards a close, Dr. Annesley asked the reader whether they could say—in the words of the psalmist—"I have kept thy precepts and thy testimonies: for all my ways are before thee" (Ps. 119:168). In order to ascertain the state of one's inner life and aspirations, the preacher posed a series of rhetorical questions, to be answered in the inner person: "What am I? What do I do? How live I? Is the course I follow good and lawful? Is that which I omit, my duty, or not? Is God my friend? Am I his? . . . What sins have I conquered now, that held me in combat then? What graces have I obtained now, that I had not then?"[22] He then urged that one should include this sort of self-examination in one's morning and evening devotions: "In the morning fore-think what ought to be done, and in the evening examine whether you have done what you ought."[23] Susanna Wesley's prayer, entitled "Seize the Opportunity," reflects the imprint of her father's spiritual disposition:

> When I examine myself three times a day, help me to do it more accurately; let no trifling matter divert me, for though it takes not much time, it is certain that opportunities once lost can never be recovered.

---

21 Samuel Annesley, ed., *The Morning-Exercises at Cripple-Gate or Several Cases of Conscience Practically Resolved, by Sundry Ministers* (London: T. Milbourn, 1661).

22 Annesley, 24.

23 Annesley, 24.

May it be that whatever my hand finds to do, I will do with all my might. When I have an opportunity, therefore, I will thankfully and vigorously make use of it, remembering that for all these things God will bring me to judgement.

Savior, I remember that when on earth you went about doing good. I must also do what good I can, especially to the souls God has committed to my care, and help me not to be discouraged by infirmities or work. Amen.[24]

The process of prayerful self-examination was passed on to the Wesley brothers, through their mother. And questions for self-examination, which were a part of the devotional practices they learned in the Epworth manse, were subsequently mirrored in the practices of the "Oxford Holy Club" and were subsequently suggested for use in the Wesleyan classes and bands, which were the backbone of the Wesleyan revival.[25] Nor was it an accident that John Wesley, "the practical theologian," would later term Christian repentance as true "self-knowledge."[26] For who can consider questions like these and not have a clearer sense of one's self (both pro and con)? This prayerful self-examination is foundational for a vital spiritual life, because it leaves us with a sense of what attitudes we need to turn *from* in order to turn more meaningfully and more completely *towards* God and God's way in the world.

Susanna Wesley's prayers illustrate very well the devotional life she planted in her children. They show her frame of mind as well as the shape of the spirituality she embraced. One representative prayer (below) is sometimes called "Susanna's Apron," because Methodist tradition associates this prayer with those difficult days in the Epworth manse when—with many challenges seemingly closing in on her—she sat in her rocking chair by the fireplace (probably one of the few personal spaces she had in the house) and pulled her apron over her head in order to transform the chaos of her family life into a private moment in God's presence:

---

24 Michael McMullen, ed., *Prayers and Meditations of Susanna Wesley* (Peterborourgh: The Methodist Publishing House, 2000), 7.

25 See, for example, "Rules of the Band-Societies," Jackson, ed., *Works of John Wesley*, Vol. III, 272–73.

26 Jackson, *Vol. I, Sermons 1,* Sermon #7, "On the Way to the Kingdom," II.1, 225.

Help me, Lord, to remember that religion is not to be confined to the church or closet, nor exercised only in prayer and meditation, but that everywhere I am in Thy presence.

So may my every word and action have a moral content. May all the happenings of my life prove useful to me. May all things instruct me and afford me opportunity of exercising some virtue and daily learning and growing toward Thy holiness. Amen.[27]

---

27 Ray Comfort with Trisha Ramos, *Susanna Wesley: Her Remarkable Life* (Alachua, FL: Bridge-Logos, 2014), 81.

Three

Methodist Methods

John and Charles Wesley were superbly equipped by the schooling they received in Susanna's kitchen, and they soon distinguished themselves at prestigious prep schools. At the tender age of ten John went off to Charterhouse School in London where he drifted into a spiritual malaise; he was outwardly religious but lacked a sense of inner power and genuine spiritual experience. He reported,

> The next six or seven years [1714–20] were spent at [Charterhouse] school; where outward retraints being removed, I was much more negligent than before of even outward duties, and almost continually guilty of outward sins, which I knew to be such, though they were not scandalous in the eye of the world. However, I still read the Scriptures, and said my prayers, morning and evening. And what I now hoped to be saved by, was (1) *not being so bad as other people,* (2) *having still a kindness for religion; and* (3) *reading the Bible, going to church, and saying my prayers.*[1]

Charles Wesley was sent off to Westminster School, also in London, where eldest brother Samuel Wesley Jr. was a tutor and became as a foster-father to young Charles, who reported that he grew up "under the care of my eldest brother Samuel, a strict Churchman, who brought me up in his

---

1   W. Reginald Ward and Richard P. Heitzenrater, eds., *The Works of John Wesley: Vol. 18, Journals and Diaries I (1735-38)* entry for May 24, 1738 (Nashville: Abingdon Press, 1988), 243.

own principles."[2] Samuel Jr. also instilled in young Charles a love for classical literature, and being a published poet himself, Samuel nurtured Charles's passion for poetry. Both would serve him well two decades later when it came time for Charles to become the "poet laureate" of Methodism.

From prep school both Wesley brothers went "up to Oxford," where they qualified for King's Scholarships at Christ Church College. John matriculated on July 18, 1720, and Charles followed him six years later in the autumn of 1726. John's diaries indicate that both Samuel and Susanna Wesley—but most especially Susanna—carried on a devotional "continuing education program" with him by correspondence during his Oxford years.[3]

Writing in the emotional high of his Aldersgate "conversion experience" of May 24, 1738, John looked back upon his spiritual state during his first five years at Oxford with discouragement and frustration. He wrote,

> For five years I still said my prayers, both in public and private, and read with the Scriptures several other books of religion, especially comments on the New Testament. Yet I had not all the while so much as a notion of inward holiness; nay, went on habitually and (for the most part) very contentedly, in some or other known sin; indeed with some intermissions and short struggles, especially before and after the Holy Communion, which I was obliged to receive thrice a year.[4]

When John reached the age of twenty-two, in 1725, his father urged him to consider whether or not he had a call to ministry, which prompted a period of reassessment and discernment. "At the same time," John recalled, "the providence of God directing me to Kempis's *Christian Pattern,* I began to see that true religion was seated in the heart and that God's law extended to all our thoughts as well as words and actions."[5] Describing the impact of this work, John reported, "The nature and extent of inward religion, the religion of the heart, now appeared to me in a stronger light

---

2 John R. Tyson, ed., "A Letter to Dr. Chandler," in *Charles Wesley: A Reader* (Oxford: Oxford University Press, 1989), 59.

3 Richard Heitzenrater, "John Wesley and the Oxford Methodists," an unpublished PhD dissertation at Duke University, 1972, 49–54.

4 Ward and Heitzenrater, eds., *Works of JW,* entry for May 24, 1738, 243.

5 Ward and Heitzenrater, 243.

than it ever had done before. I saw that giving even all my life to God . . . would profit me nothing, unless I gave my heart, yea, all my heart to Him.[6] "I saw," he continued, "that 'simplicity of intention and purity of affection,' one design in all we speak or do, and one desire ruling in all our tempers [or attitudes], are indeed 'the wings of the soul,' without which she can never ascend to the mount of God."[7] Reading Kempis helped young Wesley immeasurably by shifting his focus from outward things to the habits of his heart, but John thought that many of the specific injunctions of Kempis's were "too strict." He also found in the *Imitation of Christ* and in conversations with a new "spiritual friend," Sally Kirkham, the encouragement to begin to amend his life. "I began to alter the whole form of my conversation," he explained, "and to set out in earnest upon a new life. I set apart an hour or two a day for religious retirement. I communicated every week. I watched against all sins, whether in word or deed. I began to aim at and pray for inward holiness. So that now, *doing so much and living a good life*, I doubted not but I was a good Christian."[8]

Two years later, in 1727, while reading *A Practical Treatise Upon Christian Perfection* (1726) and *A Serious Call to a Devout and Holy Life* (1728), both by William Law (1686–1761),[9] John became convinced "more than ever, of the absolute impossibility of being half a Christian, and I determined, through His grace . . . to be all devoted to God, to give Him all my soul, my body,

---

6   J. Fred Parker, ed., *John Wesley A Plain Account of Christian Perfection* (Kansas City: Beacon Hill Press, reprint edition, 1966), 10.

7   Ward and Heitzenrater, *Works of JW*, 243.

8   Ward and Heitzenrater, 244.

9   William Law (1686–1761) was an Anglican priest who became a teaching "fellow" at College, Cambridge, in 1711. Sometime soon after that he found that his conscience would not allow him to take the oath of allegiance to King George I, the first monarch of the Hanover dynasty. A distant cousin of the English ruling house, George I was invited to come from Germany to sit upon the British throne chiefly because he was a Protestant. Many Englishmen considered King George I a usurper of the more proper line of succession which ran through the Roman Catholic House of Stuart, from Scotland. Without the oath of allegiance, "nonjurors" like Law were deprived of their teaching offices at the English Universities and unable to serve as Anglican parish priests. William Law continued to teach privately and wrote several very influential books on Christian practice and the cultivation of an inner life.

and my substance."[10] But even with this piercing spiritual insight, Wesley still thought of his relationship with God primarily in terms of the obligation to fulfill God's law and to do one's Christian duty. "I cried out to God for help," he recalled, "and resolved not to prolong the time of obeying him as I had never done before. And by my continued endeavor to keep his whole law, inward and outward, to the utmost of my power, I was persuaded that I should be accepted of Him, and that I was even then in a state of salvation."[11]

By 1729, however, John had taken to heart the core message of the *Imitation of Christ,* and he began to

> not only read, but to study, the Bible as the one, the only standard of truth, and the only model of pure religion. Hence I saw, in a clearer and clearer light, the indispensable necessity of having "the mind which was in Christ," and of "walking as Christ walked;" even of having not some part only, but all the mind which was in Him; and of walking as He walked, not only in many or in most respects, but in all things. And this was the light, wherein at this time I generally considered religion, as a uniform following Christ, an entire inward and outward conformity to our Master.[12]

It was in this sense that John Wesley described himself as *homo unis libri* ("a man of one book").[13]

Over a twenty-month period, from the summer of 1729 through the fall of 1730, John Wesley had begun to meet, informally, with two or three other young scholars for their mutual improvement in piety. These early meetings were *ad hoc* and somewhat sporadic but eventually formed the nucleus and pattern of the Oxford "Holy Club." By 1731 John had received his M.A. in classics and was elected a fellow or tutor at Lincoln College. Five or six young men began meeting in his college rooms, and by 1732

---

10 Parker, ed., *Plain Account,* 11.
11 Ward and Heitzenrater, eds., *Works of JW,* 244–45.
12 Parker, ed., *Plain Account,* 11.
13 Albert Outler, ed., *The Works of John Wesley: Sermons,* Vol. I, *Sermons 1,* "Preface to the 1746 Edition," 105.

they were being called "the Methodists."[14] John described the inception of this group:[15]

> In November, 1729, four young gentlemen of Oxford, Mr. John Wesley, Fellow of Lincoln College; Mr. Charles Wesley, student of Christ Church; Mr. Morgan, Commoner of Christ Church; and Mr. Kirkham, of Merton College—began to spend some evenings in a week together, in reading, chiefly the Greek Testament. The next year two or three of Mr. John Wesley's pupils desired the liberty of meeting with them; and afterwards one of Mr. Charles Wesley's pupils. It was in 1732, that Mr. Ingham, of Queens College, and Mr. Broughton, of Exeter, were added to their number. To these, in April was joined Mr. Clayton, of Brazen-nose [College] with two or three of his pupils. About the same time, Mr. James Hervey was permitted to meet with them; and in 1735, Mr. Whitefield.

When Charles Wesley arrived at Christ Church, Oxford, in 1726, John looked upon his younger brother as a man who "merits emulation—in meekness, tenderness, and learning."[16] Soon, however, Charles entered into a "moratorium period" of religious laxity and social experimentation, which he described somewhat furtively by saying: "My first year at College I lost in diversions."[17] Charles's "diversions," included pubbing, card playing, dancing, the theater, and gaming—all of which were large taboos in the Wesley household. More alarmingly, perhaps, was his romantic involvement with an actress—named Molly—who had previously been a "kept woman" by a local nobleman. At the same time Charles admitted he "resisted the gloomy and mechanical piety of the place."[18]

John, who had been called back to Epworth to serve as his father's curate (assistant pastor) in 1728, was quickly dispatched to Oxford to straighten out his younger brother. John sought to set his brother on a more serious path and reported that Charles "pursued his studies

---

14 Richard Heitzenrater, "The Meditative Piety of the Oxford Methodists," in *Mirror and Memory* (Nashville: Kingswood, 1989), 78–84.

15 John Telford, ed., *The Works of John Wesley*, XI, "A Short History of Methodism," 348.

16 Heitzenrater, "Oxford Methodists," 72. Quoting from the entry of John's unpublished diary for June 25, 1726.

17 Tyson, ed., *Charles Wesley*, "Letter to Dr. Chandler, April 28, 1785," 59.

18 Tyson, 59.

diligently, and led a regular, harmless life; but if I spoke to him about religion he would warmly answer, 'What! Would you have me be a saint all at once?' and would hear no more."[19] Given his mercurial temperament and stubborn nature, it is hard to imagine Charles Wesley becoming a "saint all at once." But by the end of January he had turned toward a more positive path. While an account of their earlier conversation is not extant, echoes of it are retained in Charles's letter to John, dated January 22, 1729, in which he promised: "I shall never quarrel with you again, till I am do with my religion, and that I may never do that, I am not ashamed to desire your prayers."[20] On the same note Charles reported his desire to keep a spiritual diary—which was also due to the instigation of his brother, John.

While he was away from campus in 1729, John urged his younger brother Charles to also avail himself of pious fellowship and cultivate Christian friendships with a few of his fellow students. Charles subsequently reported,

> Diligence [and John's forceful advice] led me into serious thinking. I went to the weekly sacrament, and persuaded two or three young scholars to accompany me, and to observe the method of study prescribed by the statutes of the University. This gained me the harmless nickname of Methodist. In half a year my Brother [John] left his curacy at Epworth, and came to our assistance. We then proceeded regularly in our studies, and in doing what good we could to the bodies and souls of men.[21]

Charles's recollection of the beginning of the Oxford "Methodists" hints at a division of labor based on the complementary personalities and gifts of the two brothers. Warm and spontaneous, Charles was, as his fellow student John Gambold described him, "a man made for friendship—who by the vivacity of his spirit would refresh his friends' hearts."[22] It was often his winsome personality that drew people into association with the little group, but it was John's penchant for order and organizational genius

---

19 John R. Tyson, *Assist Me to Proclaim: The Life and Hymns of Charles Wesley* (Grand Rapids, MI: Eerdmans, 2007), 9.

20 Tyson, 9.

21 Tyson, ed., *Charles Wesley*, "Letter to Dr. Chandler," 59.

22 Tyson, ed., 8.

that gave the group shape and form. This pattern of complementary and shared leadership that developed between them as "Oxford Methodists" would become the basis of a "partnership in ministry" (as they called it) that lasted more than fifty years.

The Oxford Methodists read a series of devotional classics, many of which, like *Meditations* by Bishop Ken, *Holy Living and Holy Dying* by Jeremy Taylor, and *Best Exercises* by Anthony Horneck, were embraced as "how to" lessons on prayer, meditation, and holy living.[23] A devotional classic entitled *The Life of God in the Soul of a Man* by Henry Scougal encouraged the use of small accountability groups as an aid to personal piety and devotion. It also showed them that the essence of true Christianity was and is becoming and living as a "new creation." Scougal, and the Wesleys after him, stressed the importance of the restoration of the image of God with all people; that is, the divinely given identity and righteousness each person owns as a child of God and in which all humans are created (cf. Gen. 1:26). Described as "the life of God in the soul," this process transforms one's inner life because of oneness with God, through God's Spirit. That relationship is so deep that that it causes one to become "partakers of the divine nature" (2 Peter 1:4) as godliness or Christ-likeness is formed within a person. As Scougal explained,

> They who are acquainted with [true religion] will . . . know by experience that true religion is a union of the soul with God, a real participation in the Divine nature, the image of God drawn upon the soul, or in the Apostle's phrase, "*it is Christ formed within us*" [Galatians 41:9].[24]

Charles Wesley was deeply affected by this restorative vision of Christian faith and subsequently loaned *The Life of God* to his friend, George Whitefield, who remarked, "Though I had fasted, watched, and prayed, and received the sacrament so long; yet I never knew what true religion was, till God sent me that excellent treatise by the hands of my never-to-be-forgotten friend."[25]

Through their reading of the Bible, devotional classics, and the writings of the early church leaders, the Oxford Methodists were encouraged

---

23 Heitzenrater, *Mirror and Memory*, 90.
24 Tyson, *Assist Me to Proclaim*, 230.
25 Tyson, 17.

to employ spiritual disciplines such as fasting, alms-giving, and humanitarian service; the composite picture of these and other practices they called "Primitive Christianity," perhaps borrowing the term from William Cave's book by the same title. Writing in 1673, Cave averred that he "intended to both inspire his readers and to encourage them to emulate the spiritual life and practice of the early church"; that is, "to admire and imitate their piety and integrity, their infinite hatred of sin, their care and zeal to keep up that strictness and purity of manners that had rendered their religion so renowned and triumphant in the world."[26] So enamored was John with William Cave's book, as a liturgical and practical Christian guide, that it was one of the very few personal possessions he would take with him on his Georgia mission.[27] As Geordan Hammond noted,

> Wesley's interest in catholic unity, devotional practice, moral theology, and Eucharistic theology were all aimed at his overarching concern with first understanding and then applying the practices of the primitive church. Georgia became the laboratory where Wesley implemented his vision of primitive Christianity.[28]

What the Wesley brothers learned about "Primitive Christianity" in their father's study was dramatically enhanced by their studies and fellowship with Oxford Methodists like John Clayton, who joined their group in 1732. That Primitive Christianity was also very much in the mind of Charles Wesley is illustrated by the very long hymn or poem that he published by that title in 1743. The first few verses capture and preserve well the prayerful spirit of the Oxford Methodists:[29]

---

26 William Cave, *Primitive Christianity, or the Religion of the Ancient Christians, in the First Ages of the Gospel* (London: Midwinter and Crowse, 1714), no pagination. Cited in Geordan Hammond, *John Wesley in America: Restoring Primitive Christianity* (Oxford: Oxford University Press, 2014), 22. See Hammond's fine work for a full treatment of Primitive Christianity.

27 Ward and Heitzenrater, ed., *Works of JW,* 408.

28 Hammond, *John Wesley in America,* 41.

29 For the full text see John R. Tyson, ed., *Charles Wesley: A Reader* (New York and Oxford: Oxford University Press, 1989), 185–88. The quotation above is from page 185.

Happy the souls that first believed,
To Jesus and each other cleaved;
Join'd by the unction from above,
In mystic fellowship of love.

Meek, simple followers of the Lamb,
They lived, and spake and thought the same!
Brake the commemorative bread,
And drank the Spirit of [Christ] their Head.

On God they cast their every care,
Wrestling with God in mighty prayer
They claimed the grace through Jesus given,
By prayer they shut, and open'd heaven.

To Jesus they perform'd their vow,
A little church in every house;
They joyfully conspired to raise
Their ceaseless sacrifice of praise.

One of the Oxford Methodists, John Clayton, urged his fellow students to emulate the example of the early church in close fellowship, frequent Communion, social action, and the regular observance of fasting. Under his impulse the group observed the "Stationary Fasts" on every Wednesday and Friday.[30] Charles Wesley stressed eating meatless meals—especially during Lent—while John urged "the necessity of fasting" on Benjamin Ingham and several others who were less enthusiastic about it.[31] And his correspondence with Richard Morgan suggests that John Wesley considered Morgan's desire to moderate the regiment of the Oxford Methodists by omitting fasting on Friday to be "blatantly sinful."[32] John's stringent views on fasting, however, moderated significantly over the years, as we shall see when examining his sermon on this topic in a later section.[33]

---

30 Heitzenrater, *Mirror and Memory*, 74.
31 Heitzenrater, 94.
32 Geordan Hammond, "John Wesley's Mindset at the Commencement of His Georgia Sojourn: Suffering and the Introduction of Primitive Christianity to the Indians," *Methodist History*, Vol. 47, no. 1 (Oct. 2008), 17.
33 Cf. Outler, ed., *JW Sermons, Sermons 1*, Sermon #27, 592–612.

The focal point of their fasting was to develop the habit of self-denial, or as they termed it, "mortification," which allows a person to put God and others ahead of "self." This virtue, they believed, was fundamental to all other Christian virtues, most especially matters like stewardship, temperance, and a deep gratitude for the bounty God provided in one's life. The Oxford Methodists fasted on specific days of the week, often in accordance with the Church calendar. We can see that moderation and gratitude in the partaking of food, drink, and pleasure were constants, because one of their "Resolutions for Every Day" inquired: "Have I been temperate in the desire and in the use of sensual pleasure, particularly have I been recollected [i.e. "circumspect"] and thankful in eating and drinking?"[34] In this way, fasting also provided a clearer focus for one's prayer life. It also helped a person develop deeper empathy for those who lived without regular meals and other necessities of life, an empathy that should of necessity lead to action.

Through his close study of the earliest Christians, John Clayton also pointed the Oxford Methodists to the fundamental role that a social conscious played in the life of the early church.[35] They soon began visiting the Castle Prison in order to visit, encourage, and administer the Lord's Supper to the imprisoned. This meant giving from their own meager funds to feed and clothe the poor, and it meant visiting and teaching the catechism to the poor children living at St. Thomas's workhouse, in High Bridge.[36] This synthesis of spiritual disciplines, which they would later term "works of piety," with practical humanitarian service subsequently described as "works of mercy," soon became a constant in Wesleyan spirituality.

Celebrating the Lord's Supper was another foundational aspect of the fellowship of the early church that was mirrored by the Oxford Methodists. Charles Wesley recalled that it was precisely their marching off to the weekly offered sacrament that brought the Methodists to public notice and ridicule at Oxford. George Whitefield, for example, remembered that he had to "go through a ridiculing crowd to receive the Holy Eucharist at St.

---

34 Heitzenrater, *Mirror and Memory*, 94.
35 Heitzenrater, 94.
36 Heitzenrater, 96–98.

Mary's."[37] It was about this time that John began to urge that one should receive the Lord's Supper "as often as we have opportunity," an injunction which—in practice—Benjamin Ingham thought was ridiculous, because it could mean communing as often as four or five times a day.[38] Frequent Communion, or as Wesley would later call it "constant Communion," was a Methodist spiritual emphasis from the very beginning.[39]

In the foreword to his published sermon #101, "The Duty of Constant Communion," John recalled: "The following discourse was written above five and fifty years ago, for the use of my students at Oxford . . . I thank God I have not yet seen cause to alter my sentiments in any point which is therein delivered." Wesley's first point in that sermon or discourse was characteristically direct: "I am to show that it is the duty of every Christian to receive the Lord's Supper as often as he can."[40] Not only were they following what they considered to be the command of Jesus Christ ("Do this in remembrance of me") as well as the example of the early Christians, the Oxford Methodists understood the Lord's Supper as "a means of grace" in which the risen Christ met them at his table. This meant that Communion, for them, was a transforming event, through which a person could receive spiritual encouragement and life-changing grace through faith in Jesus Christ.[41]

As their activities became more regular, the Oxford Methodists developed a pattern of piety that included Bible study, spiritual journaling, fasting, the Lord's Supper, and humanitarian service—all of which were fueled by a robust prayer life. The latter included personal (private) prayers and corporate prayer (public) by using "a form" as well as spontaneous "ejaculatory prayers" of praise and petition. The examination of one's conscience, which the Wesleys learned at home from their mother, also remained an important part of their devotional life. This emphasis is evidenced by a list

---

37 George Whitefield, *A Short Account of God's Dealings with the Reverend Mr. Whitefield* (London: Strahan, 1740), 26, in Outler, ed., *JW Sermons*, Sermons 3, Sermon #101, "The Duty of Constant Communion," 428.

38 Heitzenrater, *Mirror and Memory*, 95.

39 Outler, ed., *JW Sermons*, Vol. III, Sermon #101, "The Duty of Constant Communion," 428–39.

40 Outler, ed., 428–39.

41 More on this extremely important spiritual discipline in a subsequent chapter.

of twenty-two meditative questions, which John wrote on the inside fly-leaf of his Oxford Bible:[42]

1. Am I consciously or unconsciously creating the impression that I am better than I really am? In other words, am I a hypocrite?
2. Am I honest in all my acts and words, or do I exaggerate?
3. Do I confidentially pass on to others what has been said to me in confidence?
4. Can I be trusted?
5. Am I a slave to dress, friends, work, or habits?
6. Am I self-conscious, self-pitying, or self-justifying?
7. Did the Bible live in me today?
8. Do I give [the Bible] time to speak to me every day?
9. Am I enjoying prayer?
10. When did I last speak to someone else about my faith?
11. Do I pray about the money I spend?
12. Do I get to bed on time and get up on time?
13. Do I disobey God in anything?
14. Do I insist upon doing something about which my conscience is uneasy?
15. Am I defeated in any part of my life?
16. Am I jealous, impure, critical, irritable, touchy, or distrustful?
17. How do I spend my spare time?
18. Am I proud?
19. Do I thank God that I am not as other people, especially as the Pharisees who despised the publican?
20. Is there anyone whom I fear, dislike, disown, criticize, hold a resentment toward or disregard? If so, what am I doing about it?
21. Do I grumble or complain constantly?
22. Is Christ real to me?

The Oxford Methodists also used various instruments like this list to focus their prayers through "particular examination" in which each day was given

---

42 See https://www.umcdiscipleship.org/resources/everyday-disciples-john-wesleys -22-questions. Accessed on 9/8/2018. John Wesley later published very similar questions in his 1733 *A Collection of Forms of Prayer for Every Day in the Week*. In 1781 a list of questions like this appeared in Wesley's in the *Arminian Magazine*.

a prayerful theme that was to be carried in one's heart and mind throughout the day. One of John's early writings listed some of these:

Sunday: Love of God

Monday: Love of Man

Tuesday: Humility

Wednesday: Mortification and Self-denial

Thursday: Resignation and Meekness

Friday: Mortification and Self-denial

Saturday: Thankfulness.[43]

This prayerful spiritual pattern was replicated in John Wesley's first publication (1733) *A Collection of Forms of Prayer,* a devotional aid that represents his personal prayers along with a distillation of the *Book of Common Prayer.* It, too, was supplemented with questions for prayerful self-examination and illustrates well the spirituality of the Oxford Methodists.[44]

Building upon and supplementing the formative foundation of their Epworth years, the devotional life that the Wesley brothers experienced and developed as Oxford Methodists stayed with them life-long and provided a spiritual basis for the Methodist movement that sprung from them. Richard Heitzenrater, an expert on the Oxford Methodists, summarized their spirituality in this way:

> Their perspective embraced the simple essentials, which were grounded in the Great Commandment—to love God and to love neighbor—revealed in Scripture and epitomized in the life of Christ, which they hoped to imitate. The focus was upon nurturing the virtues basic to the Christian (Christlike) life and combating the vices that impede the development of inward holiness. This tradition, while based in Scripture, is confirmed and exemplified in Primitive Christianity; the

---

43 Heitzenrater, *Mirror and Memory,* 91.

44 See appendix A for the full text of this helpful guide.

Bible and the Early Fathers are the sources for the Oxford Methodist's thought and action.[45]

"Habits of the heart" like meditative Bible reading; attention to spiritual disciplines like the Lord's Supper, prayer (private and corporate), fasting, and purposeful humanitarian service were brought together and lived out in in the context of the support, direction, and mutual accountability of the intimate fellowship of a small group. It was in the Oxford Holy Club that the Methodists not only earned their name—but there they also found their spiritual focus and life mission.

---

45 Richard P. Heitzenrater, *Diary of an Oxford Methodist: Benjamin Ingham, 1733–1734* (Durham, NC: Duke University Press, 1985), 37.

Four

Road-Testing the Vision

The idea that the Oxford Methodists should transplant their experiment in Primitive Christianity in the wilds of Georgia must have seemed to be an exciting adventure for some of the young men, and yet for others— like Charles Wesley—it sounded utterly preposterous. Georgia had been established in 1733 as an outpost and military buffer zone between the string of British colonies that ran down the Atlantic coast of North America and the alarming appearance of Spanish military presence in nearby Florida. Spanish occupation of Florida was deemed a dire threat to British control of the region; and, ultimately, the Spanish did invade Georgia twice—in 1742 and again in 1752. There was also a humanitarian and more public side to the Georgia experiment, which was rooted in the efforts of General James Oglethorpe (1696–1785). Oglethorpe was a humanitarian, politician, and military man who clearly understood the problem that the Spanish presence in Florida posed for the government of King George II, and he tried to turn it into civic advantage.

Oglethorpe was an influential member of the British Parliament. In 1730 he served on a "blue ribbon committee" that studied an alarming increase in crime and violence in the nation's cities. A man of insight and conscience, Oglethorpe was able to see a line of connection between the criminal justice system, prisoner recidivism, and the hopelessness that drove many people to crime. His committee soon turned its attention toward the issue of prison reform as the place to begin breaking the cycle of escalating urban violence. London boasted two large prisons where people who were indebted beyond their means were incarcerated. While in prison they lost whatever means of economic support they had left in the outside world and became increasingly destitute and hopeless. Under these conditions they were very apt to turn to crime upon their ultimate release. Oglethorpe recognized that the legal process itself was criminalizing hardworking people who had experienced economic failure, and he developed a plan (which was named after him) to stem the social crisis in the cities and, at the same time, give the government a political solution to their military dilemma in the North American South.

The "Oglethorpe Plan" was simple enough: establish a British colony in Georgia and populate it with nonviolent offenders from London's debtors' prisons. By giving them a second chance in life, Oglethorpe envisioned a colony of hardworking British farmers who would seize the opportunity for a new life and put into useful production an unpopulated region with an inhospitable climate. By 1732 his plan made its way to Parliament and was signed into law by King George II. Trustees were appointed; and a strongly humanitarian charter was drawn up for Georgia, named for King George, which outlawed slavery and granted a large degree of religious liberty. German Salzburgers and Scottish Highlanders were among the numerous refugees who fled religious persecution in Europe and streamed into newly founded Georgia. The embargo on slavery changed dramatically, however, after 1752 when Georgia was taken out of the hands of the trustees, made an official "Royal Crown Colony," and placed under the direct control of the British monarchy. Consequently, native people were driven away or enslaved, and soon the plantation system migrated south from the Carolina colony—along with it the many horrors and injustices that chattel slavery inflicted upon people of African descent.

General Oglethorpe and Samuel Wesley Sr. were acquaintances, having attended Westminster School together in their youth. The father of the Wesley brothers wrote the general an enthusiastic and supportive letter on July 6, 1734, which praised Oglethorpe's plan and introduced his son, John, to him.[1] John, for his part, was in the throes of a vocational crisis; should he stay at Oxford or return to Epworth to assist his aged and infirmed father? While John had neither a deep love for nor sense of divine call to Epworth,

---

1   http://johnwesleysjournal.blogspot.com/2008/09/letter-to-gen-oglethorpe -from-samuel.html. Accessed on 9/11/2018.

the responsibility of providing a place for his aged mother and unmarried sisters, after his father's impending death, weighed heavily upon him. As the Georgia experiment generated significant interest among the Oxford Methodists, several of them—including John Wesley—were considering volunteering as missionaries there, when Samuel Wesley Sr. died on April 25, 1735.

In August of the same year, John Burton, who was a friend of John Wesley's from Corpus Christi College Oxford, and a trustee of the new Georgia Colony, began recruiting John Wesley for service there. John's manuscript journal recorded that on Aug 28, 1735 "Mr. Burton met me in Ludgate Street, and first mentioned Georgia to me. After a conference or two with Mr. Oglethorpe on that subject, on Monday, Sept. 1, I returned to Oxford."[2] The "call" to Georgia, however, left John Wesley in a dilemma relative to the care of his recently widowed mother and his sisters. It was resolved, in part, by his mother's selfless and enthusiastic support for John's desire to go to Georgia; "Had I twenty sons," Susanna declared, "I should rejoice that they were all so employed, though I should never see them more."[3]

Surviving correspondence between John Wesley and Dr. Burton indicates that the latter assumed that Wesley's chief motivation for accepting the mission to Georgia was "to do good to the souls of others, and in consequence to that of your own." Wesley's subsequent statement about his own sense of failure regarding his work in Georgia suggests that John may have reversed the order of Dr. Burton's two aims for him in his own thinking. It was as a forlorn and frustrated young missionary that Wesley wrote: "I went to America to convert the Indians, but Oh! Who shall convert me?"[4] For his part, Dr. Burton also offered young pastor Wesley pragmatic and practical advice urging him to use "Christian prudence" in order to "distinguish between what is essential and merely circumstantial to Christianity" and to avoid the temptation that many fall into by trying to enforce "the traditions and ordinances of men . . . with

---

2   Nehemiah Curnock, ed., *The Journal of John Wesley, A.M Standard Edition* 8, Vol. (London: Charles Kelley, 1916), 8:151.

3   Henry Moore, *The Life of John Wesley, A.M.* in 2 vol. (New York: 1826), Vol. I:234.

4   W. Reginald Ward and Richard P. Heitzenrater, eds., *The Works of John Wesley: Vol. 18, Journals and Diaries I* (1735–38) (Nashville: Abingdon Press, 1988), 211.

more zeal than the weighty matters of God's law." Burton had in mind, as Geordan Hammond noted, precisely the sort of missionary-pastor Georgia needed; one, who like the apostle Paul, could become "all things to all people."[5] But John received rather mixed reviews regarding his work in Georgia; some of his parishioners "remembered him as a legalistic High Churchman; some, criticized him for narrow minded austerity, while others praised him for [his] consistent efforts to care for their physical and spiritual needs."[6]

Charles Wesley, on the other hand, described his own path to Georgia quite differently: "I took my Master's Degree," he wrote, "and only thought of spending all my days at Oxford. But my brother [John], who had always had the ascendant over me, persuaded me to accompany him and Mr. Oglethorpe to Georgia. I exceedingly dreaded entering into holy orders; but he overruled me here also, and I was ordained Deacon by the Bishop of Oxford, Dr. Potter, and the next Sunday, Priest, by the Bishop of London, Dr. Gibson."[7] If Charles heard the voice of God in this "call" to Georgia, it sounded a lot like the voice of his elder and often domineering brother, John.

The Georgia mission became an opportunity to "road test" the spirituality developed by the Oxford Methodists. Two of their college companions, Benjamin Ingham (1712–72) and Charles Delamotte (1714–96), accompanied the Wesley brothers to the New World. "Our end in leaving our native country was not to avoid want (God having given us plenty of temporal blessings), nor to gain the dung or dross of riches or honor," John recalled, "but singly this—to save our souls, to live wholly to the glory of God."[8] They lightened the burden of their four-month transatlantic voyage by continuing the spiritual regiment of the Oxford Methodists

---

5   Geordan Hammond, "John Wesley's Mindset at the Commencement of His Georgia Sojourn: Suffering and the Introduction of Primitive Christianity to the Indians," *Methodist History*, Vol. 47, no. 1 (Oct. 2008), 18. Alluding to the apostle's statement in 1 Cor. 9:19–23.

6   Geordan Hammond, "John Wesley in Georgia: Success or Failure?" in *Proceedings of the Wesley Historical Society*, Vol. 56, 300.

7   John R. Tyson, ed., *Charles Wesley: A Reader* (New York: Oxford University Press, 1989), 59.

8   Ward and Heitzenrater, eds., *Works of JW*, 136.

and by assuming pastoral duties for their fellow travelers. Perhaps the most interesting among the group were twenty-six German-speaking Moravians with whom the Wesleys, particularly John, soon struck up a formative friendship.

The Moravians were descendants of the Lutheran tradition who embraced the inward emphases of German Pietism. This synthesis caused them to embrace Luther's concept of justification by faith alone, while also insisting that saving faith was a "faith that you feel." A soul-searching conversation between John Wesley and the Moravian Bishop August Spannenberg (1704–92) illustrates this well. John's journal recorded: "Have you the witness within yourself?" Spannenberg asked. "Does the Spirit of God bear witness with your spirit that you are a child of God?" Wesley recalled, "I was surprised and knew not what to answer. He observed it, and asked, 'Do you know Jesus Christ?' I paused, and said, 'I know he is the savior of the world." Spannenberg replied, "True, but do you know he has saved you?" Wesley answered, "I hope he has died to save me." Spannenberg added, "Do you know yourself?" "I do," Wesley answered, but he "fear[ed] they were vain words."[9]

John's journal reported a second aspect of Moravianism, with which he became enamored. While standing upon the open deck of the ship in the midst of a howling gale, they turned to congregational song for comfort and strength. "In the midst of the psalm wherein their service began the sea broke over, split the mainsail in pieces, covered the ships, and poured in between the decks, as if the great dead had already swallowed us up," he recalled. "A terrible screaming began among the English [passengers]. The Germans calmly sung on. I asked one of them afterwards, 'Was you not afraid?' He answered, 'I thank God, no.' I asked, "but were not your women and children afraid?' He replied mildly, 'No, our women and children are not afraid to die.'"[10]

This shining example of the spiritual power of congregational song was not lost on the Wesley brothers; John employed it in his pastoral role in Georgia, where he compiled and published the first hymnbook

---

9   Ward and Heitzenrater, eds., 146.
10   Ward and Heitzenrater, eds., 143.

printed in North America in 1737.[11] Charles, for his part, supplied the early Methodists with more than 9,000 hymns and sacred poems.[12] During the Wesleyan revival, which was still more than a decade away, popular hymnody became the prayer book, Bible commentary, and catechism for the working poor who embraced Methodism. As British Methodist, J. Earnest Rattenbury, explained: "His hymns gave wings to the doctrines of their Evangelical Revival, so that they flew everywhere; their personal emotional character disseminated truth as no other medium could have."[13] Using more modern parlance, one might say that with the emergence of the popular corpus of Wesleyan hymns early Methodism's message "went viral."

The spiritual life that the Wesleys sought to develop among themselves and their parishioners in Georgia was in many ways a continuation of what had begun in the Epworth manse and had been enhanced in their student days at Oxford. This is made clear by the list of observances John drew up while crossing the Atlantic on the *Simmonds*:[14]

> I believe it *myself* it is a duty to observe, so far as I can *without breaking communion with my own church*:
>
> 1. To baptize by *trine* immersion.
> 2. To use water *mixed with wine*, Oblation of Elements *i.e. present the elements as a sacrificial offering*, Alms, a Prothesis *a table of preparation of the elements*, Invocation *of the Holy Spirit on the elements* in the Eucharist.
> 3. To pray for the Faithful Departed.
> 4. To pray standing on Sunday and in Pentecost.
> 5. To observe Saturday and Sunday Pentecost as a festival.
> 6. To abstain from Blood, things strangled.

---

11 Cf. John Wesley, ed., *A Collection of Psalms and Hymns* (Charleston: Lewis Timothy, 1737).

12 Cf. Tyson, ed., *Charles Wesley,* "The Hymns," for an examination of Charles Wesley's productivity as a lyricist, 20–29.

13 J. Ernest Rattenbury, *The Evangelical Doctrines of Charles Wesley's Hymns* (London: Epworth Press, 1941), 15.

14 This list was developed by John Wesley by drawing upon a book of devotions by Rev. Thomas Deacon. The portions printed in italic, above, were Wesley's editorial additions. Cf., 55.

I think it prudent *our own Church not considered*:

1. To observe the Stations i.e. *stationary fasts*.
2. Lent, especially the Holy Week.
3. To turn to the East at the Creed.

On the very first Sunday that John Wesley conducted public worship in Savannah, John told his parishioners,

> (1) That I must admonish every one of them not only in public, but from house to house; (2) That I could admit none to Holy Communion without previous notice; . . . (6) That in general, though I had all the ecclesiastical authority which was entrusted to any within this Province, yet I was only a servant of the Church of England, not a judge, and therefore obliged to keep her regulations in all things.[15]

Ironically, John's energetic preaching, his rigorous spiritual regiment, and his pastoral diligence caused others, like Captain Dunbar and Rev. William Norris (who succeeded Wesley in Savannah) to view John as "an enthusiast," which—in eighteenth-century parlance—described someone whose zeal for religion was excessive, extravagant, and unbalanced, a religious "nut."

The small group practice of the Oxford Methodists also followed John and Charles to Georgia. By April 1736, John and his colleagues

> agreed first, to advise the more serious among them ["the flock at Savanah"] to form themselves into a sort of little society, and to meet once or twice a week, in order to reprove, instruct and exhort one another; second, to select out of these a smaller number for more intimate union with each other, which might be forwarded, partly by our conversations singly with each, and partly by inviting them all together to our house; and this accordingly we determined to do every Sunday in the afternoon.[16]

At least 185 of these meetings were held during Wesley's tenure in Savannah, and they followed the same general pattern of opening and closing

---

15 Geordan Hammond, *John Wesley in America: Restoring Primitive Christianity* (Oxford: Oxford University Press, 2014), 110.

16 Ward and Heitzenrater, eds., *Works of JW,* Vol. I, entry for April 17, 1736, 157.

with singing, followed by a devotional reading and prayers. John gave a fairly exact accounting report of their practices in a letter to Dr. Bray (February 1737): "Sometime after the [Sunday] Evening Service, as many of my parishioners as desire it meet at my house (as they do likewise on Wednesday evening) and spend about an hour in prayer, singing, reading a practical book, and mutual exhortation."[17]

John Wesley's high churchman's approach to worship caused the local justice, Thomas Causton, to charge him with being "a Papist, if not a Jesuit."[18] But when John became romantically involved with Causton's niece, Sophy Hopkey, and then afterward, when the couple had a falling out, excluded her from Communion (based on rule #2 above) the wheels came off Wesley's Georgia experiment. His misuse of ecclesiastical authority (obviously John saw it otherwise) led to charges being filed against him for defamation of character, which caused Wesley to leave Georgia in a hurry and in disgrace.

Charles's Georgia experience was much briefer than John's. It was tinged with a sadness born in serious illness and a strong sense of having failed at what he set out to do: "The hardship of lying on the ground, and etc., soon threw me into a Fever and Dysentery, which in half a year forced me to return to England. My brother returned the next year. Still we had no plan, but to serve God, and the Church of England."[19]

The primitive conditions of life in a frontier outpost certainly were a large factor in Charles's predicament, so also was his inability to negotiate the challenges of small town gossip and the animosity of those (like Mrs. Hawkins and Mrs. Welch) who actively sought to undermine him and his ministry. The women managed to drive a wedge of suspicion between the younger Wesley and General Oglethorpe, which, while it was eventually overcome, made Charles's life and work very unpleasant. After a period of intercessory prayer for those who opposed him, by meditating over the Bible Charles found the spiritual guidance and strength he needed to continue his work. He wrote,

---

17 Frank Baker, ed., *The Works of John Wesley*, Vol. 25, Letters, I (Oxford: Clarendon, 1980), 495.

18 Hammond, *Primitive Christianity*, 116.

19 Tyson, ed., *Charles Wesley*, "Letter to Dr. Chandler," 59.

After breakfast, I again took myself to intercession, particularly for Mrs. W[elch], that Satan, in the shape of that other bad woman [Mrs. Hawkins], might not stand at her right hand. . . . I consulted the oracle [that is, the Bible], and met Jeremiah 44:16, 17—"as for the word which thou has spoken to us in the name of the Lord, we will not hearken unto it; but we will certainly do whatsoever thing goeth forth out of our own mouth." This determined me not to meddle with them at all.[20]

Assessments of John Wesley's ministry in Savannah vary greatly. In John's own mind, particularly as he looked back in the afterglow of his subsequent Aldersgate experience, it looked to be an utter failure. His stated goal of ministering to the indigenous people did not happen, and his own spiritual fiber was sorely tested and found desperately wanting—by his own standards. And so, it was a discouraged and defeated young man who wrote,

I went to America to convert the Indians, but Oh! Who shall convert me? Who, what is he that will deliver me from this evil heart of unbelief? I have a fair summer religion. I can talk well, nay, and believe myself, while no danger is near. But let death look me in the face, and my spirit is troubled. Nor can I say [with St. Paul] "to die is gain."[21]

John's melancholy words have too often been taken at face value, as if to prove that his Georgia mission was, by all standards, an utter failure. But clearly this was not the case. One of his parishioners, Philip Thickness, who was not a supporter of John Wesley, reported that "his deportment in public [was] grave and ready, his language pure, and his preaching captivatingly persuasive."[22] General James Oglethorpe, Wesley's supervisor, also gave a complimentary assessment: "The Change since the Arrival of the Mission is very visible, with respect to the Increase of Industry, Love and Christian Charity among them."[23]

---

20 Tyson, *Charles Wesley*, 69. This is Charles's journal entry for March 24, 1736.
21 Ward and Heitzenrater, eds., *Works of JW*, Vol. 18, 211, entry for Jan. 24, 1738.
22 Rodney M. Baine, "Notes and Documents: Philip Thickness's Reminisces of Early Georgia," *Georgia Historical Quarterly* 74, no. 4 (Winter 1990), 690.
23 Allen D. Candler, ed. *The Colonial Records of the State of Georgia* (Atlanta: Chas. Byrd, 1910), Vol. 21, 198.

How shall we account for the discrepancy between the outer assessment by Wesley's contemporaries, which was quite favorable, and his own sense of disappointment and utter failure? Clearly, we see here the impact of that process of prayerful self-examination, learned at his mother's knee. Wesley and his colleagues, while falling short of their stated aim of converting the Indians, had tangible success in many other aspects of their work. But John's vision was also focused within, on his inner person, because he was concerned (and might we say "overly concerned") about what this experience taught him about his own spiritual state. Wesley looked deeply inside himself and found himself sadly wanting.

The searing light of self-examination can and should be seen as both a good and a bad thing. One the one hand, it was clear to John, in the words of a contemporary slogan, "God was not done with him—yet." There was much more inner, spiritual work to be done in him. In this case, Wesley's discipline of self-examination put him in a mental and spiritual place that taught him that he needed to make some significant changes in his life with God. On the other hand, such an exaggerated and frank self-assessment was depressing, debilitating, and painful. It should have been counterbalanced by the outer and more favorable one. John should have been able to say: "We did a good job," or "We did the best we could for God," while also recognizing that inwardly he was still not the person that either he or God wanted him to be. But John and Charles Wesley were, in this case, both poignant examples of how even a "wounded healer," though not entirely whole, is able to do good work for God and for God's people, even while she or he continues to struggle and grow in grace.

Five

Born in Crisis

Like many faith traditions, Methodist spirituality was born in crisis. We have already explored the religious and political turmoil that preceded and surrounded the life and work of the Wesley brothers. To this needs to be added a profound economic shift and social dislocation that brought multitudes of rural people to the new, burgeoning industrial cities of England in search of employment and a better way of life. The promise of economic prosperity proved to be elusive for many, and droves of people wound up working for low, stagnant wages that kept them locked into poverty and hopelessness. The Wesleys called these people "the working poor"; even as these people broke their backs doing hard labor, they sunk deeper and deeper into poverty. Because they left the safety net of their extended family in the rural locales, these same people experienced utter hopelessness and isolation.

John and Charles returned to England from Georgia with a crisis of their own. Charles had a deep melancholy that was born of serious and repeated illness and fueled by his sense of vocational indirection. For John, failure in Georgia was even more shattering, because, in his mind, it pointed to a serious inner deficiency in his understanding of faith and acceptance before God. However, both brothers, under the tutelage of Moravian friends and missionaries, experienced heartwarming encounters with God in May 1738. Charles met God afresh on his sickbed on Pentecost Sunday, May 21, because one of his nurses (Mrs. Musgrave) came into his sickroom while Charles was in prayer and challenged him with the words: "In the name of Jesus of Nazareth, arise, and believe, and thou shalt be healed of all thy infirmities."[1] To make a long story short: Charles did, and so did Jesus. By the next day Charles was feeling much better and shared his newfound faith with visitors. He also began writing hymns celebrating his new life in Christ. Among the more famous of these early "conversion hymns" was one entitled "Free Grace," which is now more often known by its first line:

> And can it be, that I should gain,
> an interest in the Savior's blood!
> Died he *for me*?—who caused his pain!
> *For me*?—who him to death pursued?
> Amazing love! How can it be
> that thou, my God, shoulds't die *for me*?
>
> . . . .
>
> Long *my* imprison'd spirit lay,
> fast bound in sin and nature's night;
> thine eye diffused a quickening ray;
> I woke; the dungeon flamed with light;
> *My* chains fell off, *my* heart was free,
> *I rose*, went forth, and follow'd thee.[2]

That this song, like most of Charles's hymns, was born in his own spiritual life and experience is clearly evidenced by its strong first-person language: "I, for me, my" that resounds throughout. The hymn is a testimony of a faith experience as well as a celebration of it. But the Wesleyan hymns were not only celebrations of religious experiences, they are also—by putting the language of praise and freedom upon the lips of the singer—able to *induce* the singer to join in the same experience.

John Wesley's more famous "Aldersgate Experience" occurred three days later on May 24, 1738. Where Charles's hymns described a heart set free, John's experience was one of going from feeling "a strange indifference, dullness, and coldness" to this affirmation: "My heart was strangely

---

1   John R. Tyson, ed., *Charles Wesley: A Reader* (New York and Oxford: Oxford University Press, 1989), 98.

2   See *The United Methodist Hymnal* (Nashville: The United Methodist Publishing House, 1989), 363, verses 1 and 4 with emphasis added.

warmed. I felt that I did trust in Christ, Christ alone for salvation, and an assurance was given me that he had taken away *my* sins, even *mine*, and saved *me* from the law of sin and death."[3] Once again the first person language is significant; John no longer thought only of Jesus dying for the "sins of the world"; he now received profound personal, inner assurance that Christ died "for me." Not surprisingly, this new realization became the focal point of Wesleyan evangelism, both in sermon and song, as John and Charles sought to explain to a broken world that through faith in Christ you can feel and find a holy love that both frees and transforms the inner person. John described their new understanding of the life of faith in terms of doing one's duty, as opposed to living out our loving family relationships. It was like having the faith of a "servant" of God—following orders and doing one's duty—and then subsequently joyously discovering that one was a member of the family (and not just "hired help"); hence could and should live freely and spontaneously as "a son" or child of God. As "a child of God" one feels accepted and affirmed as a member of God's loving family and is able to live out one's life with "the spirit of child-like love" for God.[4]

More surprising than the potency of this message, and its resonance among the common people who heard it, was the increasingly negative reception the Wesleys' proclamation received in the Anglican churches of London and elsewhere. They soon found themselves "excluded from the churches" and compelled to embark upon the innovation of "field preaching." John recalled,

> In a short time, partly because of those unwieldy crowds, partly because of my unfashionable doctrine, I was excluded from one and another church, and at length shut out of all. Not daring to be silent, after a short struggle between honor and conscience I made a virtue of necessity and preached in the middle of Moorfields. Here were thousands upon thousands, abundantly more than any church could

---

3   W. Reginald Ward and Richard P. Heitzenrater, eds., *The Works of John Wesley: Vol. 1, Journals and Diaries I* (1735–38) (Nashville: Abingdon Press, 1988), 250.

4   Albert Outler, ed., *The Works of John Wesley: Sermons*, IV (Nashville: Abingdon Press, 1987), Sermon 110, "On the Discoveries of Faith," for example, 35.

contain; and numbers among them who never went to any church or place of public worship at all.[5]

The multitudes who heard the Wesleys preach were not, at that point, considered "Methodists." Instead they became Methodists as they learned and lived out the "method" of spirituality in the close fellowship and supportive environment of small accountability groups called "classes" and "bands."

Drawing upon their home-life and Oxford experience, the Wesley brothers soon formed a network of small groups of intentional disciples who responded to the message of heartwarming faith and liberating, transforming love. These Methodist "classes" became the locus for forming and shaping people's broken lives into a consistent life of faith. Because of their social location among the working poor, the regiment of Methodist classes included spiritual disciplines, or "works of piety," as well as real-world humanitarian service or "works of mercy."[6] These included a poor box, loan fund, Bible society, and a dispensary for supplying medicine. John Wesley even compiled and prescribed the latest home remedies in his layman's guide to medicine, *The Primitive Physick* (1747).[7]

These small groups of ten to twelve people, who lived in the same neighborhood, were broadly inclusive; social location, gender, education level, economic status, and race did not matter. Class membership was based solely upon "a desire to flee from the wrath to come, and to be saved from their sins"; but these earnest desires were also expected to take shape in concrete actions:

> First, by doing no harm, and by avoiding evil in every kind; . . . secondly,
> by doing good, by being, in every kind. Merciful after their power; as
> they have opportunity, doing good of every possible sort, and as far as is

---

5   Outler, ed., *JW Sermons*, III, Sermon #112, "On Laying the Foundation of the New Chapel," 583–84.

6   Outler, ed., *JW Sermons*, I, #14, 343, and #26, 573–74 for a discussion of "works of piety" and "works of mercy."

7   John Wesley, *The Primitive Physick or an Easy and Natural Method for Curing Most Diseases* (London: Strahan, 1761); Wesley first published it anonymously in 1747. The full text of this work is available at https://www.umcmission.org/Find-Resources/John-Wesley-Sermons/The-Wesleys-and-Their-Times/Primitive-Physick.

possible, to all men—to their bodies . . . to their souls . . . and by denying themselves, and taking up their cross daily.[8]

The third stipulation for continuing in the fellowship of the classes and bands was a willingness to embrace: "ministry of the word, either read, or expounded; the supper of the Lord; family and private prayer; searching the Scriptures; and fasting or abstinence."[9]

The aim and practices of these small groups were described in the "Rules of the Band-Societies," drawn up by the Wesleys and the preachers associated with them at the Christmas Conference of 1738—just seven months after the brothers' heart experiences. "The design of our meeting, the Rules state, is to obey that command of God, 'Confess your faults one to another and pray for one another, that ye may be healed,' [Jas. 5:16]."[10] Hence, while the meeting included close fellowship, instruction, and celebration, spiritual formation and the healing of the inner person were the primary goals.

The group process used by the classes echoed the regimen that was learned in the Epworth manse and refined by the Oxford Methodists:[11]

1. To meet once a week, at the least.
2. To come punctually at the hour appointed, without some extraordinary reason.
3. To being . . . exactly at the [appointed] hour with singing or prayer.
4. To speak each of us in order, freely and plainly, the true state of our souls, with the faults we have committed in thought, word, or deed, and the temptations we have felt, since our last meeting.
5. To end every meeting with prayer, suited to the state of each person present.

---

8   Thomas Jackson, ed., *The Works of John Wesley, A.M.*, 14 vols., Vol. VIII, "The General Rules," 270–71.
9   Jackson, 271. More will be said about these spiritual disciples in a subsequent chapter.
10 Jackson, 272.
11 Jackson, 272.

6. To desire some person among us to speak his own state first, and then to ask the rest, in order, as many and as searching questions as may be, concerning their state, sins, and temptations.

In our mind's eye, perhaps, we can see an earnest group of Christians singing, praying, and testifying together in deep fellowship and in the context of deep personal relationships; forged, no doubt, through months and months of these weekly meetings. In the Rules we also detect a strong emphasis on pastoral care and spiritual formation, practiced in the context of loving and accepting Christian friends.

This group process revolved around an "examination of conscience," which was a large part of the spirituality and prayer life of Susanna Wesley and her illustrious father, and it echoed the soul-searching questions that John Wesley had written into the flyleaf of his Oxford Bible. Among these were the following:[12]

1. Have you the forgiveness of your sins?
2. Have you peace with God, through our Lord Jesus Christ?
3. Have you the witness of God's Spirit with your spirit, that you are a child of God?
4. Is the love of God shed abroad in your heart?
5. Has no sin, inward or outward, dominion over you?

Some of the questions the Wesleys suggested for these sessions show how deeply confession, forgiveness, and transformation (through amendment of life) were all wrapped up in the process of healing souls. Hence the members were encouraged to ask or answer questions such as these: "Do you desire to be told your faults?" and "Is it your desire and design to be on this, and all other occasions, entirely open, so as to speak everything that is in your heart without exception, without disguise, and without reserve?"[13] These questions, and others like them, suggest a level of intimacy and trust that is rare among Christians today. And yet, they remind us that, either inwardly or outwardly, we—as practitioners of the life of faith—need to be asking them of ourselves and others we love. It also seems, while we may not reach this level of spiritual transparency in a small group of Christian

---

12 Jackson, 272.
13 Jackson, 272.

believers—we need to find this level of both acceptance and accountability from a few close Christian friends.

John Wesley's own prayer life is legendary. It is well known that he rose early in the morning, 4:00 a.m., to pray and meditate for an hour. He also enjoined a similar pattern on his preachers, asking them, "Do you use private prayer every morning and evening? If you can, at five in the evening . . . Do you forecast [plan for it] daily, wherever you are, how to secure these hours? Do you avow it everywhere? Do you ask everywhere, 'Have you family prayer?'"[14] Recognizing that early rising does not come easily to everyone, he also drew up and published instructions on how a person could become accustomed to rising early for prayer.[15] He was utterly convinced that the neglect of prayer, particularly private prayer, led directly to a "wilderness state" in the soul in which the "life of God" within us begins to "decay" and "gradually die away." John explained,

> Nothing can be more plain than that the life of God in the soul does not continue, much less increase, unless we use all the opportunities of communing with God, and pouring out our hearts before him. If therefore we are negligent of this, if we suffer business, company or any avocation whatever, to prevent these secret exercises of the soul . . . that life [of God] will surely decay. And if we long or frequently intermit them, it will gradually die away.[16]

John tried to maintain formal prayer times three times a day, and he sometimes prayed "by a form"—such as the *Book of Common Prayer* or another resource. As they emerged, the Methodist hymns also became a "prayer-starter" for the early Methodists and their hymnbooks. For example, the "big" hymnbook of 1780 offered entire sections of hymns "For Believers Praying."[17] But prayer, in the larger sense, was to become a way of life for the early Methodists. Following the injunction, "Pray without ceasing . . . [and] give thanks" (1 Thes. 5:17-18), they understood their entire lives

---

14 Jackson, 322–23.

15 Outler, ed., *JW Sermons*, III, #93, "On Redeeming the Time," 330–31.

16 Outler, ed., *JW Sermons*, II, #46, "The Wilderness State," 209.

17 Franz Hildebrandt and Oliver Beckerlegge, ed. *The Works of John Wesley* Vol. VII, *A Collection of Hymns for the Use of the People Called Methodists* (Nashville: Abingdon, 1983), 346–50.

as an ongoing, prayerful conversation with God. Prayer was to be the chief "business" of the Christian disciple, who sang: "My business this, my only care, My life, my every breath be prayer!"[18] Indeed, prayer is to become as natural for us as breathing:

> Prayer and thanksgiving is the vital breath
> That keeps the spirit of man from death;
> For prayer attracts into the living soul
> The life that fills the universal whole;
> And giving thanks is breathing forth again,
> The praise of Him who is the life of man.[19]

---

18 Hildebrandt and Beckerlegge, #96, 202.

19 Hildebrandt and Beckerlegge, Vol. XII, "Letter DLXII," 482.

Six

Means of Grace

The "Methodist methods," or spiritual disciplines, that were practiced in the close fellowship of small groups—classes and bands—were the spiritual engine that propelled the movement forward as well as being (arguably) its most distinctive aspect. Looking at the example laid down in Jesus's "Sermon on the Mount" (Mt. 6:1-15), John Wesley drew upon and broadened the phraseology of the Anglican tradition to describe Christian life in a twofold pattern of practice, which encompassed "works of piety" and "works of mercy." While he acknowledged that all religious "works" are indifferent—neither good nor bad in their basic nature—each can become "good and acceptable to God, by a pure and holy intention, before God."[1]

Wesley described "works of piety" as "those which are usually accounted religious actions and are performed with a right intention"[2] Among the "works of piety" that Jesus described in his sermon in Matthew 6, prayer stood in the forefront. "Prayer," John wrote, "is the lifting up of the heart to God: all words of prayer without this are mere hypocrisy. Whenever therefore thou attemptest to pray, see that it be thy one design to commune with God, to pour out thy soul before him."[3] Among the several evocative phrases Wesley employed to define authentic prayer,

---

1   Albert Outler, ed., *The Works of John Wesley: Sermons* #26: "Upon our Lord's Sermon on the Mount, part VI," (Nashville: Abingdon Press, 1987), 573.

2   Outler, ed., *JW Sermons*, 573.

3   Outler, ed., 575.

"lifting up the heart" and "pour out thy soul" seem particularly instructive, since they describe prayer that is heartfelt and passionate as well as an unrestrained, and in that sense, utterly honest expression of one's deepest concerns.

"Works of mercy," again following Jesus's sermon, were described as "feeding the hungry, the clothing the naked, the entertaining or assisting the stranger, the visiting those that are sick or in prison, the comforting the afflicted, the instructing the ignorant, the reproving the wicked, the exhorting and encouraging the well-doer."[4] Here John Wesley seemed to be blending the text from the "Sermon on the Mount" with Jesus's parable from Matthew 25, where Jesus detailed a disciple's responsibility and care for those whom Jesus described as "the least of these my brethren" (Mt. 25:40).

The spiritual experiences of both Wesley brothers, in May 1738, taught them to distinguish clearly between the two main aspects of Christian salvation: justification and sanctification. "Justification by faith," John noted, "as another word for pardon. It is the forgiveness of all our sins, and . . . our acceptance with God."[5] Sanctification, however, begins immediately after "justification," or "pardon" in Wesleyan soteriology:

> At the same time that we are justified, yea, in that very moment, sanctification begins. In that instant we are "born again," "born from above," "born of the Spirit." There is *a real* as well as a *relative change*. We are inwardly renewed by the power of God. We feel the "love of God shed abroad in our heart by the Holy Ghost which is given unto us."[6]

An intellectual inversion of justification and sanctification had proved disastrous for both Wesley brothers. It set them on a path of trying to earn God's acceptance through good deeds and holy attitudes, causing them to embark upon living a life of duty and obligation, which John described as "the life of a servant." After May 1738, however, they came to see that having received God's "free grace" as pardon, they could and did live a life of faith that was characterized by joy and freedom in God's

4   Outler, ed., 573.
5   Outler, ed., *JW Sermons*, I, #43, "The Scripture Way of Salvation," 157.
6   Outler, ed., 158.

acceptance—which John described as "the life of a son" or the life of a child of God.

Charles put the issue more pointedly one day when he visited Rev. William Law, several of whose books had dramatically shaped the lives and faith of both Wesley brothers. "I told him," Charles recalled, "that he was my schoolmaster to bring me to Christ, but the reason why I did not come sooner to Him was my wanting to be sanctified before I was justified."[7] While good works play *no* role in a person's justification or acceptance before God, when performed in faith they *do* play a part in one's sanctification. Hence, while faith in Christ is the only basis for justification and sanctification, "the practice of all good works, works of piety, as well as works of mercy . . . are in some sense necessary to sanctification."[8] Just as a conscientious musician or athlete must practice her or his craft to become and remain proficient, so also is the life of faith honed and enhanced by regular practice. It was precisely this recognition of the innerconnection of faith and good works that became the impetus for the Methodist emphasis upon five main spiritual disciplines, which, borrowing from the Church of England, they termed "the means of grace."

In his sermon by that title, John defined "the means of grace" as "outward signs, words, or actions ordained by God, and appointed for this end—to be the *ordinary* channels whereby he might convey to men preventing [or 'prevenient'], justifying, or sanctifying grace."[9] While it is eminently clear that "Christ is the only means of grace,"[10] in the proper sense, the Methodist spiritual disciplines are esteemed as promised and effective means for meeting Christ, the Incarnated and Exalted Source of God's grace. It was for this reason, then, that the "Large Minutes," which guided the life and practice of the early Methodist classes, bands, and societies, asked the early Methodist preachers and members: "Do you

---

7   S. T. Kimbrough and Kenneth Newport, eds., *The Manuscript Journal of the Reverend Charles Wesley, M.A.*, 2 vol. (Nashville: Kingswood, 2018), I:184, entry for August 10, 1739.

8   Outler, ed., *JW Sermons*, I, #43, "The Scripture Way of Salvation," 164.

9   Outler, ed., #16, "The Means of Grace," 381.

10   Outler, ed., #16, 383.

use all the means of grace yourself, and enforce the use of them on all other persons?"[11]

Those "minutes of some late conversations between the Rev. Mr. Wesleys and others," divided the means of grace into two categories of spiritual practice, "the instituted" and "prudential" means. The five disciplines that were termed "instituted" were understood as coming to the Christian with both God's command to "Do this," as well as God's promise that God would be graciously met through using them. The much longer list of "prudential means" were those wise (e.g. "prudent") practices, whereby a conscientious person of faith might "grow in grace" and practice the "arts of holy living."[12] First among the five "instituted" means of grace is prayer: "private, family, public, consisting of deprecation, petition, intercession, and thanksgiving." In his sermon #16, in a rhetorical dialogue with someone who disagreed with this terminology, John explained in what sense the Methodists esteemed prayer as "a means of grace": "When *we* say, 'prayer is a means of grace,' we understand a channel through which the grace of God is conveyed. When *you* say, 'Christ is the means of grace,' you understand the sole price and purchase of it; or that 'no man cometh unto the Father, but through him.' And who denies it?"[13]

In short, the Wesleys understood prayer as a profound encounter and connection with God in Christ, a connection that can be grace-bearing. Prayer, as "an instituted" means, was established through Jesus's words "Pray like this" (Mt. 6:9 CEB), which the early Methodists received as a divine directive.

After stating the discipline and giving some suggestions about how to practice prayer, the "Large Minutes" went from description to prescription by asking the Methodist: "Do you use private prayer every morning and evening? If you can, at five in the evening . . . ? Do you forecast daily, wherever you are, how to secure these hours [to pray]? Do you avow it everywhere? Do you ask everywhere, 'Have you family prayer?'"[14] The emphasis upon "family prayer" here almost certainly hearkens back to those distant

---

11 Jackson, ed., *Works of John Wesley*, Vol. VIII, 322.
12 Jackson, ed., 323.
13 Outler, ed., *JW Sermons*, VIII, 323; #16, "The Means of Grace," 391.
14 Jackson, ed., *Works of John Wesley*, VIII, 323.

days in the Epworth manse where the entire Wesley family learned to pray under Susanna's direction.

Next comes "Searching the Scriptures" by reading and meditating upon them. Once again the injunction received directly from Jesus's words: "Search the scriptures; for in them ye think ye have eternal life: and they are they which testify of me" (Jn. 5:39), which were accorded divine authority. And here the "Large Minutes" give clear directions regarding "how" to read the Bible: "*constantly*, some part of every day; *regularly*, all the Bible in order; *carefully*, with the Notes; *seriously*, with prayer before and after; *fruitfully*, immediately practicing what you learn there."[15] One should also be reading the Bible by *prayerfully*, reflectively "meditating" over it. The "Minutes" also ask: "At set times? By any rule?"[16] "Hearing" the scriptures read was also stressed as an important spiritual discipline. Again the "Minutes" addressed the practitioner with a series of pointed questions: "Every morning? Carefully; with prayer before, at, after; immediately putting in practice? Have you a New Testament always about [i.e. "with"] you?"[17]

The third instituted means of grace, and probably the one we are most apt to think of, is the Lord's Supper. Jesus's words: "Do this in remembrance of me" (Lk. 22:19; 1 Cor. 11:24 NRSV) also sounded like a holy obligation to the early Methodists. In his sermon "The Duty of Constant Communion," John urged "it is the duty of every Christian to receive the Lord's Supper as often as [she or] he can. The first reason why it is the duty of every Christian so to do is because it is a plain command of Christ . . . 'Do this in remembrance of me.' "[18] Charles's "Eucharistic Hymn #84" captured well this same emphasis:

> Jesus hath spoke the word,
> His will my reason is;
> *Do this* in memory of Thy Lord,
> Jesus hath said, *Do this!*
>
> He bids me eat the bread,
> He bids me drink the wine;

---

15 Jackson, ed., *Works of John Wesley*, VIII, emphasis added.

16 Jackson, ed., 323.

17 Jackson, ed., 323.

18 Outler, ed., *JW Sermons*, III, #101, "The Duty of Constant Communion," 428.

No other motive, Lord, I need,
No other word than Thine.[19]

While no theory of Christ's presence or our reception of him is offered, the life-giving influence of the Holy Spirit "infuses" Christ's love into "every faithful heart":

Come, Holy Ghost, Thine influence shed,
And realize the sign;
Thy life infuse into the bread,
Thy power into the wine.

Effectual let the tokens prove,
And made, by heavenly art,
Fit channels to convey Thy love,
To every faithful heart.[20]

The "Minutes" also offer a series of practical questions that shape the use of the sacrament: "Do you use this at every opportunity? With solemn prayer before; with earnest and deliberate self-devotion?"[21] The importance of Holy Communion is easily seen in the Wesleys' willingness—following the lead of the early church—to esteem it as both a *converting* and *confirming* ordinance. Calling Communion a "converting ordinance" reminds us that God's Holy Spirit is present with the elements to call people to repentance and faith; and, therefore, to Christian salvation, and those who already have faith in Christ can, through participation in the Lord's Supper, have their faith both confirmed and strengthened.[22]

Fasting, sometimes identified as "abstinence" in other places, comes next on the list with the inquiry: "How do you fast every Friday?"[23] Jesus's

19 John Wesley, ed., *Hymns on the Lord's Supper*, #84, verses 4 and 5. Reprinted here from John R. Tyson, ed., *Charles Wesley: A Reader* (New York and Oxford: Oxford University Press, 1989), 282.

20 Eucharistic Hymn #52, reprinted from Tyson, ed., *Charles Wesley,* 281.

21 Jackson, ed., *Works of John Wesley,* VIII, 323.

22 Cf. W. Reginald Ward and Richard P. Heitzenrater, eds., *The Works of John Wesley: Journals and Diaries*, Vol. 19, Journals and Diaries I–VII (Nashville: Abingdon, 1988–2003), 157–58, for these terms.

23 Jackson, ed., *Works of John Wesley,* VIII, 323.

words, "*when* you fast" (Mt. 6:16 CEB), assumed that one would indeed already be fasting, as opposed to Jesus saying "*if* you fast," as though it were not a holy obligation. John Wesley noted several reasons why a person should embrace the discipline of fasting. The most notable of these was to practice self-discipline or self-denial, both of which are cardinal virtues for the life of faith. And it helps one, Wesley opined, to "withdraw the incentives of foolish and hurtful desires, of vile and vain affections."[24] The chief reason to fast, however,

> is that it is a help to prayer. . . . It is chiefly as it is a help to prayer that it has so frequently been found a means in the hand of God of confirming and increasing not one virtue . . . but also seriousness of spirit, earnestness, sensibility, and tenderness of conscience; deadness to the world, and consequently the love of God and every holy and heavenly affection.[25]

And, finally, the Large Minutes urge upon us "Christian conference," or a close fellowship shaped around spiritual conversation, sharing, and instruction. Once again, the pattern of the earliest Christians provided both the incentive and the model for this spiritual discipline: "They devoted themselves to the apostles' teaching and fellowship, to the breaking of bread and the prayers. . . . And all who believed were together and had all things in common" (Acts 2: 42, 44 NRSV). The example of the Primitive Church was both the impetus and example for the Methodist classes. Charles's hymn, "Primitive Christianity," shows how deeply the Wesleys embraced the importance of this kind of close Christian fellowship:

Happy the souls that first believed,
To Jesus and each other cleaved;
Join'd by the unction from above,
In mystic fellowship of love.

Meek, simple followers of the Lamb,
They lived, and spake, and thought the same!
Brake the commemorative bread,
And drank the Spirit of their Head.

---

24 Outler, ed., *JW Sermons*, I, "Sermon on the Mount VII, 600.
25 Outler, ed., 600.

On God they cast their every care,
Wrestling with God in mighty prayer
They claim'd the grace through Jesus given,
By prayer they shut, and open'd heaven.

To Jesus they performe'd their vow,
A little church in every house;
They joyfully conspired to raise
Their ceaseless sacrifice of praise.[26]

The "Means of Grace" were the lifeblood of the early Methodist societies. These five spiritual disciplines gave inner strength and staying power to small, dedicated groups of Christian disciples scattered throughout England and later elsewhere, including America. The spiritual energy they generated and the transformation they brought in the hearts and minds of those women and men fueled and fired the Wesleyan revival, which mobilized people from all walks of life to join in the task of making a better world—or in Wesley's words—help Methodists spread "Scriptural holiness across the land."

Charles's long hymn, entitled "The Means of Grace," describes the joy and efficacy of these spiritual disciplines as channels of God's forgiveness and love. This hymn was written as both a response and correction to the Wesleys' early tendency to "trust in" the ordinances of God because of a sense of duty, rather than using these spiritual disciplines as an avenue to meet their gracious God in Christ:

Thou bidd'st me search the Sacred Leaves,
And taste the hallow'd Bread:
The kind commands my soul receives,
And longs on Thee to feed.

Still for Thy loving kindness, Lord,
I in Thy temple wait;
I look to find Thee in Thy word,
Or at Thy table meet.

---

26 "Primitive Christianity," first published in 1743, in 30 verses. It was shortened and edited by John for republication in the "Big" Collection of Hymns of 1780. The verses above are 1–4, from Charles's original version, reprinted from Tyson, ed., *Charles Wesley*, 185.

Here, *in Thine own appointed ways,*
I wait to learn Thy will:
Silent I stand before Thy face,
And hear Thee say, "Be Still!"

"Be still—and know that I am God!"
'Tis all I live to know;
To feel the virtue of Thy blood,
And spread it praise below.

I wait my vigour to renew,
Thine image to retrieve,
The veil of outward thing pass through,
And grasp in Thee to live.

I work, and own the labour vain,
And *thus* from works I cease;
I strive, and see my fruitless pain,
Till God create my peace.

Fruitless, till Thou Thyself impart,
Must all my efforts prove:
They cannot change a sinful heart,
They cannot purchase love.

I do the thing Thy laws enjoin,
And *then* the strife give o'er;
To Thee I *then* the whole resign;
I *trust* in means no more.

I trust in Him who stands between
The Father's wrath and me;
JESU! Thou great eternal Mean,
I look for all from Thee.[27]

---

27 "The Means of Grace," first published in the Wesleys' *Hymns and Sacred Poems*, 1739. It is reprinted here from Tyson, ed., *Charles Wesley*, 267–69. The verses above are numbers 12–20 of Charles's original 23.

The Methodist "means of grace" are a door to Christ and a pathway to Christian living; a designated place to encounter God—a place appointed by God precisely for that purpose. Because they believed they could meet God in Christ through prayer, scripture study, the Lord's Supper, fasting, and fellowship, Methodists highly esteemed and used these means as a channel through which God's love and grace can be poured afresh into their lives.

Seven

A More Excellent Way to Pray

It should come as no surprise that when John Wesley described "the More Excellent Way"[1] to live, he placed great importance upon the practice of prayer. He typically thought of prayer as being practiced in three forms: "private, family and public."[2] This short list begins in the inner person and reaches out to the ever-broadening world of our lives, relationships, and concerns. After stressing the importance of rising at an early hour in order to pray, John turned his attention to the question of *how* to pray. His own upbringing and Anglican context were evident in John's observation that

> the generality of Christians, as soon as they rise, are accustomed to use some kind of prayer; and probably to us the same form still which they learned when they were eight or ten years old. Now I do not condemn those who proceed thus . . . as mocking God, though they have used the same form without any variation, for twenty or thirty years together.[3]

While not condemning those who used formal, repetitious prayers—because at least these people *are* actually praying—Wesley addressed himself to the suitability of this rote approach. He asked: "But surely there

---

1   Albert Outler, ed., *The Works of John Wesley: Sermons* #89, "The More Excellent Way," Vol. III, 263–77.
2   Thomas Jackson, ed., *The Works of John Wesley, A.M.*, 14 vol. (Grand Rapids, MI: Baker Book House, 1986); see Vol. VIII, "Minutes," 322.
3   Outler, ed., *JW Sermons*, Vol. I, 267.

is a more excellent way of ordering our *private* devotions?"[4] Clearly, the answer to Wesley's rhetorical question is yes, but then how?

John's first suggestion was borrowed from his former spiritual mentor, "that great and good man" Rev. William Law, who urged those who pray to take stock of their "outward and inward state."[5] This amounts to a broader and more comprehensive application of the "examination of conscience," which the Wesleys learned from their maternal grandfather by way of their mother. If your outward state is "prosperous"—and here John was not thinking chiefly in monetary terms—but "you are in a state of health, ease, and plenty, having your lot cast among kind relations, good neighbors, and agreeable friends," then quite clearly your "outward state" should, upon reflection, generate a profound sense of gratitude, which "calls for prayers that begin with much "praise and thanksgiving to God."[6] If, on the other hand, you are "in a state of adversity," such as "poverty, in want, in outward distress," "imminent danger," or "pain and sickness," then you should "pour out your soul before God in such prayer as is suited to your circumstances."[7]

In a similar way, one's devotions should also take stock of one's true "inward state." If you are in "a state of heaviness either from a sense of sin or through manifold temptations," your prayer should break out of rote patterns and give voice to these needs. Hence, Wesley suggested: "Let your prayer consist of such confessions, petitions, and supplications, as are agreeable to your distressed situation of mind."[8] The phrase "pour out your soul before God" describes well this preparatory step. It reminds us that true prayer is heartfelt conversation between our deepest self and God, our Creator, and Parent. And, since prayer is actually a "conversation," it is well to remember that the process of pouring out one's soul before God must include *a time of listening* for God's "still small voice" of love, acceptance, assurance, affirmation, and sometimes conviction to echo back in the inner person. Wesley also urged that our devotional time should be augmented with "a little reading and meditation, and perhaps a psalm of praise." All in

---

4   Outler, ed., 268. Emphasis added.
5   Outler, ed., 268.
6   Outler, ed., 268.
7   Outler, ed., 268.
8   Outler, ed., 268.

all, a more excellent way to pray is to understand and practice prayer as the "natural effusion of a thankful heart."[9] This approach, Wesley rightly opined, "is a more excellent way than the poor dry form which you used before."[10]

If one would ask the Wesleys for a model for prayer, they would readily point us to the example Jesus provided for us in the "Our Father," or "Lord's Prayer," which John described as "a divine form of prayer" that was "proposed by way of pattern . . . as the model and standard of our prayers."[11] And John's extensive exposition of the Lord's Prayer in his sermon #27, "On Our Lord's Sermon on the Mount, pt. 6," is formative and helpful devotional reading.[12] As we noted earlier, Wesley urged his hearers to join "works of piety" with "works of mercy" so that our hearts and hands work in unison.[13] So he urged that it was "a bad idea to ask God to do something that you were not willing to do yourself,"[14] echoing the same sentiment.

John Wesley divided the Lord's Prayer into three main parts: "the preface, the petitions, and the doxology or conclusion." The first part, "the preface," amounts to us calling to mind to *Whom* we are speaking "before we can pray in confidence of being heard." That is to say, we should take stock of Who God is to us, individually and as a body of believers, even as we take stock of ourselves (as above) when we begin to pray. Clearly, there is much to say about who God is to us, but here John would have us think of God as:

1) *Creator and preserver* of our life and those we love, "Who sustains the life he has given" and in "Whose continuing love we now and every moment receive life and breath, and all things." For "in him we live, and move, and have our being" (Acts 17:28).

2) *Giver of mercy* to whom we can boldly turn for "help in times of need." It is precisely for this reason we should "pour out our soul before God" in "confessions, petitions, and supplications, as are agreeable to your distressed situation of mind."[15]

---

9   Outler ed., 268.
10 Outler, ed., 268.
11 Outler, ed., 268.
12 Outler, ed., #26, "Upon Our Lord's Discourse on The Sermon on the Mount: Discourse The Sixth," Vol. I, 572–91.
13 Outler, ed., 573
14 Outler, ed., 573.
15 Outler, ed., 573.

3) *Father of our Lord Jesus Christ.* This aspect calls to mind God's role as our Redeemer, who freely accepts, justifies, and adopts into God's forever-family, God's very own daughters and sons by faith. It is well to remember that God who is our Father or Parent is also and supremely the Father of our Lord Jesus Christ, and indeed a close reading of Jesus's words shows us that his relationship with God was at the same time absolutely unique and yet also the pattern for our own.

4) *Healer of our infirmities.* God who created us in God's own image, the *imago dei* (in terms of our inner state and nature) also heals the brokenness and distortions of our created identity as children of God.

5) *Giver of new life.* Who as poured "the Spirit of his Son into our hearts . . . saying 'Abba, Father,' Who hath 'begotten us again of incorruptible seed,' and 'created us anew in Christ Jesus.'"[16] In short, clearly understanding *Who* God is and *what* God has done and is doing for and in us helps us pray with great love and gratitude: "We pray because we love. And 'we love him because he first loved us' [1 Jn. 4:19]."[17]

Of the six petitions or requests of the Lord's Prayer, the first three: 1) "Hallowed be thy name"; 2) "Thy kingdom come"; and 3) "Thy will be done" pertain to the true worship of God in our hearts and the acceptance God's reign and will in our lives. The next three requests: 4) "Give us this day our daily bread"; 5) "Forgive us our debts"; and 6) "Lead us not into temptation" are about us and the necessities of our lives, be they spiritual or physical. Wesley clearly stressed the corporate or collective aspect of these three petitions. It is not just *my* daily bread but *our* daily bread and not merely *my* debts but *our* debts, and in fact we ask (somewhat fearfully, I hope) that God would forgive us "even as *we* forgive others." In each case the prayer both affirms and emphasizes the deep interconnection that unites all the children of God in our collective needs and concerns.

The final request, "Lead us not into temptation, but deliver us from evil" asks God's protection and guidance in all things spiritual and physical. Our tendency to associate this "temptation" primarily with our sin or sins is probably a mistake. The terminology here suggests that "temptation" in

---

16 See, for example, John 8:38, 56 and 20:17.

17 Outler, ed., *JW Sermons*, Vol. I, 579. Wesley's phraseology borrows from Psalm 103:3, Gal. 4:6, and 1 Thes. 5:17, among other scripture texts.

this sense affirms the much larger project of reclamation, which begins with alleviation from temptation and sins and then goes far beyond it. Hence, "lead us not into temptation" in this place, is probably better translated more broadly "to mean [deliver us] from trial of any kind."[18]

The last segment of the Lord's Prayer, our model prayer, John Wesley described as a "doxology"; that is, "a solemn thanksgiving, a compendious acknowledgement of the attributes and works of God."[19] It asks that God's everlasting power and love reign in us and in our world. It looks to God's "executive power" to govern and remake our world, our lives, and own dilemmas and even to bring good out of the apparent evil that all so often seems to encompass us. These aspects, God's kingdom, will, and power are indeed tangible signs and manifestations of God's "glory" among us. To which we say, "Amen," or "So be it."[20]

As if to remind us of the intersection of prayer and hymns of praise, John concluded his discourse on the Lord's Prayer with a hymn entitled "A Paraphrase on the Lord's Prayer," which may serve better as an act of prayer and meditation than a congregational song:[21]

Father of all, whose powerful voice
Called forth this universal frame,
Whose mercies over all rejoice,
Through endless ages still the same.
Thou by Thy word upholdest all;
Thy bounteous LOVE, to all is showed,
Thou hear'st Thy every creature call,
And fillest every mouth with good.

In heaven Thou reign'st, enthroned in light,
Nature's expanse beneath Thee spread;
Earth, air, and sea before Thy sight.

---

18 Outler, ed., 579.
19 Outler, ed., 587.
20 Outler, ed., 589.
21 First published in the Wesleys' *Hymns and Sacred Poems*, 1742 edition. It is not clear whether this poem was written by Charles or John Wesley. Their typical pattern was that Charles composed the lyrics, while John edited and published them, but that was by no means true in each and every case.

And hell's deep gloom are open laid.
Wisdom, and might, and love are Thine,
Prostrate before Thy face we fall,
Confess Thine attributes divine,
And hail the sovereign Lord of all.

Thee, Sovereign Lord, let all confess
That moves in earth, or air, or sky,
Revere Thy power, Thy goodness bless,
Tremble before Thy piercing eye.
All ye who owe to Him your birth,
In praise your every hour employ;
Jehovah reigns! Be glad, O earth,
And shout, ye morning stars, for joy.

Son of Thy Sire's eternal love,
Take to Thyself Thy mighty power,
Let all earth's sons Thy mercy prove,
Let all Thy bleeding grace adore.
The triumphs of Thy love display;
In every heart reigns Thou alone,
Till all Thy foes confess Thy sway,
And glory ends what grace begun.

Spirit of grace, and health, and power,
Fountain of light and love below,
Abroad Thine healing influence shower,
O'er all the nations let it flow.
Inflame our hearts with perfect love,
In us the work of faith fulfill;
So not heaven's hosts shall swifter move
Than we on earth to do Thy will.

Father, 'tis Thine each day to yield
Thy children's wants a fresh supply;
Thou cloth'st the lilies of the field,
And hearest the young ravens cry:
On Thee we cast our care; we live
Through Thee, who know'st our every need;

O feed us with Thy grace, and give,
Our souls this day the living bread.

Eternal spotless Lamb of God,
Before the world's foundation slain,
Sprinkle us ever with Thy blood;
O cleanse and keep us ever clean.
To every soul fall praise to Thee!
Our bowels of compassion move,[22]
And all mankind by this may see
God is in us; for God is love.

Giver and Lord of life, whose power
And Guardian care for all art free;
To Thee in fierce temptation's hour
From sin and Satan let us flee.
Thine, Lord, we are, and ours Thou art;
In us be all Thy goodness show'd;
Renew, enlarge and fill our heart
With peace, and joy, and heaven, and God.

Blessing and honor, praise and love,
Co-equal, co-eternal Three,
In earth below, in heaven above,
By all Thy works be paid to Thee.
Thrice holy, Thine the kingdom is,
The power omnipotent is Thine,
And when created nature dies,
Thy never-ceasing glories shine.[23]

---

22 The phraseology here, which strikes the modern reader as being quite odd, is a quotation from 1 John 3:17, which reflects the use of "bowels" in the Hebrew Scriptures to describe the deepest part of a person or God (cf. Ps. 22:14, 71:6; Isaiah 16:11, 63:15; Jeremiah 31:20; and Lamentations 1:20, for example).

23 William Osborn, *The Poetical Works of John and Charles Wesley*, 13 vols. (London: Methodist Conference, 1872), Vol. II, 335–37, with spelling and punctuation modernized.

While not forsaking or completely laying aside his Anglican heritage of praying "by a form" or prepared resources, for example the *Book of Common Prayer*, the early Methodists stressed a "more excellent way" to pray that replaced rote repetition with a spontaneous outpouring of the human heart, which was well attuned to the inward and outward circumstances of our lives. Because we pray in full recognition of *Who* God is to us, and *what* God has done *for* and *in* us and others, this becomes a very effective approach to prayer which is nothing more or less than the "natural effusion of a thankful heart."[24]

---

24 Outler, ed., *JW Sermons*, Vol. III, 268.

Eight

Elements of Wesleyan Prayer

Prayer, in the Wesleyan tradition, is esteemed as "a means of grace." This phrase identifies prayerful communion with God as a way to experience God's presence, forgiveness, and acceptance. While in the strictest sense "Christ is the only means of grace,"[1] a person is able to encounter Jesus Christ through prayer in life-giving ways. John Wesley described prayer as an opportunity in which we are "called to pour out your soul before God,"[2] and because we pray in deep awareness of God's gracious love and provision for us, prayer "is natural effusion of a thankful heart."[3] Prayer was enjoined upon the early Methodists in three basic forms: "private, family, and public";[4] of these, "private prayer," or personal devotions, was most emphatically stressed as the foundation and spiritual reservoir for the others. Without our own prayer life well intact our prayerful life or ministry with our families, friends, and congregants lacks sufficient roots. Put simply, it is very difficult to give others something that we lack ourselves.

In his sermon #46, "The Wilderness State," John Wesley used Israel's dry and precarious trek through the Sinai desert as a metaphor for our loss of spiritual life and dynamism through trial, temptation, willful disobedience,

---

1   Albert Outler, ed., *The Works of John Wesley: Sermons* #16, "The Means of Grace," 382.
2   Outler, ed., *JW Sermons*, I, #89, "The More Excellent Way," 268.
3   Outler, ed., 268.
4   Jackson, ed., *Works of John Wesley*, Vol. VIII, 322.

and sheer neglect. After the children of Israel had been delivered from their bondage in Egypt (a symbol of salvation), they came "into a 'waste and howling desert,' where they are variously tempted and tormented. And in some . . . have termed 'a wilderness state.'" Cataloguing the impact and emotional texture of this negative experience, Wesley described it as a *loss of love* within, because

> the Spirit no longer "witnesses with their spirits that they are the children of God" [Rom. 8:16]; neither does he continue as the Spirit of adoption, "crying in their hearts, Abba, Father" [Gal. 4:6]. They have not now a sure trust in his love, and a liberty of approaching him with holy boldness . . . They are [like Samson of old] shorn of their strength, and become weak and feeble-minded, even as other men [Cf. Judges 16:7, 11, 19].[5]

This loss of love engenders a loss of "*true, living faith*. . . . They are not now happy in God, as everyone is that truly loves him."[6] And, "in consequence of the loss of faith and love follows, thirdly, *loss of joy* in the Holy Ghost. For if the loving consciousness of pardon be no more, the joy resulting therefrom cannot remain. If the Spirit does not witness with our spirit that we are the children of God, the joy that flowed from that inward witness must also be at an end."[7]

In a similar way, "with the loss of faith and love and joy there is also joined fourthly, the loss of that *peace* which once passed all understanding. That sweet tranquility of mind, that composure of spirit, is gone. Painful doubt returns . . ."[8] "But even this is not all," Wesley continued, "for loss of *peace* is accompanied with *loss of power*. We know everyone who has peace with God through Jesus Christ has power over all sin. But whenever he loses the peace of God he loses also the power over sin."[9] The prevailing term in this litany woe is "loss"; loss of love, living faith, peace, and spiritual power—yes, that's a lot to lose!

---

5 Outler, ed., *Sermons of John Wesley*, II, #46, "The Wilderness State," 206. Emphasis added.

6 Outler, ed., 206. Emphasis added

7 Outler, ed., 207. Emphasis added.

8 Outler, ed., 207. Emphasis added.

9 Outler, ed., 207–8. Emphasis added.

Willful disobedience of God's will and God's way in the world were the most obvious causes of the spiritual malady John Wesley described as "the wilderness state."[10] But sins of neglect or "sin of omission" were also among the culprits that robbed Christians of spiritual health. Chief among these, he said, was

> the neglect of private prayer; the want [i.e., "lack"] whereof cannot be supplied by any other ordinance whatever. Nothing can be more plain that the life of God in the soul does not continue, much less increase, unless we use all the opportunities of communing with God, and pouring out our hearts before him.[11]

Writing like one who had heard all the excuses before, John warned,

> If we suffer ["allow"] business, company, or any avocation whatever, to prevent these secret exercises of the soul (or which comes to the same thing, to make us hurry them over in a slight and careless manner), that life will surely decay. And if we long or frequently intermit them, it will gradually die away.[12]

He could not be clearer that he viewed the neglect of private prayer as the highway to spiritual dryness, the loss of all comforting Christian virtues and, ultimately, to death within.

John Wesley provided several lists of the specific elements that comprise effective prayer; the most comprehensive of these described prayer as "consisting of deprecation, petition, intercession, and thanksgiving."[13] This fourfold delineation may have been based upon the phraseology of 1 Timothy 2:1 (KJV), which described the elements of prayer as: "supplications, prayers, intercessions, and giving of thanks." Wesley's term, "deprecation," is an archaic way of describing the purifying effect of searing self-examination, as one who looks closely at one's life and inner-self she or

---

10 Outler, ed., 208–9.

11 Outler, ed., 209.

12 Outler, ed., 209.

13 Origen of Alexandria (185–254), who was one of the first pastor-theologians to write comprehensively on prayer, also characterized effective prayer as being comprised of four elements, though these were not identical to those described by John Wesley.

he finds many things "to deplore" or "disapprove of."[14] This quite naturally impels the sensitive soul to confession and repentance. So, in the larger theological sense, "deprecation" describes an inner assessment that leads to "confession." "Petition" describes the requests (typically for oneself) that are brought before God for reply and resolution. The scripture text from 1 John 5:15 evidences the deep interconnection between deep faith and the ability to both ask and receive: "And if we know that he hear us, whatsoever we ask, we know that we have the petitions that we desired of him." "Intercession" describes petitions or prayers on behalf of others, as in Romans 15:30, where Paul prayed on behalf of the church in Rome. That the Holy Spirit helps Christians know how to make these requests is evident from Romans 8:26-27: "The Spirit also helpeth our infirmities: for we know not what we should pray for as we ought: but the Spirit itself maketh intercession for us with groanings which cannot be uttered. And he that searcheth the hearts knoweth what is the mind of the Spirit, because he maketh intercession for the saints according to the will of God."

Psalm 100:3-4 captures well the Wesleyan inner connection of praise and thanksgiving: "Know ye that the LORD he is God: it is he that hath made us, and not we ourselves; we are his people, and the sheep of his pasture. Enter into his gates with thanksgiving, and into his courts with praise: be thankful unto him, and bless his name." "Thanksgiving" describes the "effusion of a thankful heart," and the praise one offers God for God's faithfulness to the one who prays.

A slightly different list of the elements of prayer appeared in John's sermon, "The More Excellent Way," in which "supplications" were added immediately after "petitions" instead of "thanksgiving."[15] This does not seem to be an exact equivalent because "supplications," while suggesting gratitude, more often refers to a "plea, entreaty, or appeal,"[16] which carries overtones of being both a request and a doxology (an act of thanksgiving). Psalm 28:6 demonstrates the connection between praise and

---

14 Dictionary.com, s.v. "deprecate (*v. used with object*)," https://www.dictionary.com /browse/deprecation. Accessed on 10/28/18.

15 Outler, ed., *JW Sermons*, III, #89, "The More Excellent Way," 268.

16 Outler, ed., *JW Sermons*, II, 268, https://www.bing.com/search?q=supplications%20 meaning&pc=cosp&ptag=G6C999N1234D010118A98C4AF66BD&form=CONMH P&conlogo=CT3210127. Accessed 10/28/18.

thanksgiving quite well when the psalmist prayed, "Blessed be the LORD, because he hath heard the voice of my supplications."

While prayer in the Wesleyan tradition has often been shaped by great texts from Scripture and Christian devotional classics, John Wesley urged a "more excellent way" to pray that embraced formal, prepared prayers and went beyond them. He wanted to go beyond rote adherence in order to also give voice "to the natural effusion of a thankful heart."[17] As John Wesley noted in one of his later sermons: "As I know no forms that will suit all occasions, I am often under a necessity of *praying extempore*."[18] Wesley's private diaries (as opposed to his public published journals) reveal the fabric of a prayer life that is woven out of the regular use of the *Book of Common Prayer*—notably the aids for "Morning and Evening Prayer," as well as extemporaneous "ejaculatory prayers." The latter, odd-sounding, archaic term, describes "an abrupt emphatic utterance or exclamation";[19] and in that sense it is a good description of what he had in mind regarding "praying extempore." These were "short sentence prayers that would usually take just a few minutes."[20] They were often full of raw emotion.

Following Paul's injunction in 1 Thes. 5:17, "Pray without ceasing," the Wesleys practiced an additional and more spontaneous form of extemporaneous prayer.[21] This amounted to living one's life as an ongoing conversation with God. John described this approach as "a command" of God,[22] but it is born in the depths of a loving relationship as opposed to an overt sense of duty. His approach speaks to the spontaneous and "natural effusion of a thankful heart."[23] John described prayer's motivation when he wrote: "We pray because we love. And we love him because he first loved

---

17 Outler, ed., *JW Sermons*, I, #89, The More Excellent Way," 268.

18 Outler, ed., *JW Sermons*, IV, #121, "Prophets and Priests," 81.

19 Dictionary.com, "ejaculation (*n.*)" https://www.dictionary.com/browse/ejaculation. Accessed 10/30/18.

20 J. Reginald Ward and Richard P. Heitzenrater, eds., *The Works of John Wesley: Vol. 18, Journals and Diaries I, (1735–1738)*, 305.

21 So prominent was this approach in their spiritual life that the standard works of John alone, evidence almost 150 occurrences of that phrase.

22 Outler, ed., *JW Sermons*, I, #25, "Sermon on the Mount, pt. V, 555.

23 Outler, ed., *JW Sermons*, III, #89, "The More Excellent Way," 268.

us."[24] Indeed, in the Wesleys' view, approaching all of life as prayer was endemic to *The Character of a Methodist*:

> For indeed he "prays without ceasing." It is given him "always to pray and not faint." Not that he is always in the house of prayer; though he neglects no opportunity of being there . . . But at all times the language of his heart is this: "Thou brightness of eternal glory, unto thee is my heart, though without a voice, and my silence speaketh unto thee." And this is true prayer and this alone. But his heart is ever lifted up to God, at all times and in all places.[25]

The Wesleyan hymn, "The Whole Armour of God," described this same spontaneous and ongoing prayer as a way to keep our defensive "armour bright" through "constant care." It was most likely Charles Wesley who wrote:

> Pray, without ceasing pray
> (Your Captain give the word).
> His summons cheerfully obey,
> And call upon the Lord;
> To God your every want
> In instant prayer display;
> Pray always, pray, and never faith;
> Pray, without ceasing pray.[26]

Recalling the Wesleyan emphasis upon the deep interconnection between "works of piety"—spiritual disciplines, including prayer—and "works of mercy"—deeds of love and humanitarian service—it is probably not too surprising to find that John Wesley urged "all that a Christian does . . . is prayer." He wrote:

---

24 Outler, ed., *JW Sermons*, I, "Sermon on the Mount, pt. VI," 579.

25 Jackson, ed. *Works of John Wesley*, Vol. VIII, 343. The full text of this marvelous tract is available at https://www.umcmission.org/Find-Resources/John -Wesley-Sermons/The-Wesleys-and-Their-Times/The-Character-of-a-Methodist. Accessed 10/30/18.

26 Franz Hildebrandt and Oliver Beckerlegge, eds., *The Works of John Wesley Vol. VII, A Collection of Hymns for the Use of the People Called Methodists* (Nashville: Abingdon, 1983), #259, v. 4, 401.

All that a Christian does, even in eating and sleeping, is prayer, when it is done in simplicity, according to the order of God, without either adding to or diminishing from it by his own choice. Prayer continues in the desire of the heart, though the understanding be employed on outward things. In souls filled with love, the desire to please God is a continual prayer.[27]

Here, Wesleyan spirituality connects the life of prayer with the larger vision of Christian stewardship (or vocation). Commenting upon Luke 16:2, "Give an account of thy stewardship; for thou mayest no longer steward," John reminded his listeners,

We are indebted to him [God] for all we have; but although a debtor is obliged to return what he has received . . . [The steward] is not at liberty to use what is lodged in his hands as he pleases, but as his master pleases. . . . Now this is exactly the case of every man with relation to God.[28]

Where we modern readers may be tempted to link "stewardship" most directly to the financial aspects of discipleship, true stewardship runs much deeper and broader; it assumes that there is nothing in our lives that is "indifferent," since all has been given to us by God and is to be used for God's purposes. This includes our soul, our mental powers and will, as well as our goods and bodies, which we are "fearfully and wonderfully made" [Ps. 100:3] "with all the powers and members thereof."[29] The employment of all aspects of ourselves as well as our time and abilities are to be met and manifested through the prayerful deployment of our "worldly goods." How should this be done? Wesley asked. He imagined the Lord telling his steward that after "first supplying thy own reasonable wants, together with those of thy family; then restoring the remainder to Me, through the poor"[30] What a powerful statement! In it is found in the assertion that we can restore our bountiful resources to God by putting them into the service of the poor among us! In this broader sense of stewardship, John imagined the Lord asking each of us soul-searching questions:

---

27 Jackson, ed., *Works of John Wesley*, Vol. XI, "A Plain Account of Christian Perfection," 438.

28 Outler, ed., *JW Sermons*, II, #51, "The Good Steward," 283.

29 Outler, 285.

30 Outler, 285, capitalization changed for clarity.

Wast thou accordingly a general benefactor to mankind? Feeding the hungry, clothing the naked, comforting the sick, assisting the stranger, relieving the afflicted according to their various necessities? Wast thou eyes to the blind, and feet to the lame? A father to the fatherless, and an husband to the widow? And didst thou labor to improve all outward works of mercy, as means of saving souls from death?[31]

That certainly gives us a picture of the comprehensive nature of our own stewardship, as well as John Wesley's interpretation of the scripture text urging us to "give account of thy stewardship."

Charles Wesley's hymn/prayer, "Before Work," captures the interconnection between prayerful consecration to God and our "daily labor," which epitomizes Wesleyan spirituality and allows us to see all of life as an act of prayer:

Forth in thy name, O Lord, I go,
My daily labor to pursue,
Thee, only thee, resolved to know
In all I think, or speak, or do.

The task thy wisdom has assigned
O let me cheerfully fulfil,
In all my works thy presence find,
And prove thy acceptable will.

Thee may I set at my right hand
Whose eyes my inmost substance see,
And labor on at thy command,
And offer all my works to thee.

Give me to bear thy easy yoke,
And every moment watch and pray,
And still to things eternal look,
And hasten to thy glorious day;

For thee delightfully employ
Whate'er thy bounteous grace hath given,

---

31 Outler, 285.

And run my course with even joy,
And closely walk with thee to heaven.[32]

Prayer in the Wesleyan tradition is comprised of deprecation (confession), petitions, intercession, and thanksgiving, with "supplications" also joining the list on some occasions. Private prayer is stressed as the foundation for an authentic spiritual life, without which one falls into "the wilderness state," which is essentially a life of death. Alongside and in addition to formal times and well-thought-out approaches to prayer, the Wesleys stressed that one should "pray without ceasing," or offer short "ejaculatory prayers," which are nothing more than the spontaneous reaction of a faithful heart to one's own inner or outer history. John's detailed exposition of "that model prayer," the Lord's Prayer, advised that we should embark upon prayer with a strong sense *to Whom* we are speaking and *what* it is the Lord requires of us, that is: "to do justice, and to love kindness, and to walk humbly with your God" (Mic. 6:8).

The Wesleyan interconnection between "works of piety" and "works of mercy" leads us to a consideration of prayer itself in the larger context of our Christian life and vocation as stewards of ourselves, our talents, gifts, and skills—all for our improvement unto sanctification and to the improvement of others. Hence we are urged to join "the desires of our hearts to the efforts of our hands."

---

32 John Wesley selected this hymn from Charles's *Hymns and Sacred Poems*, 1749 for inclusion in his "big" hymnal of 1780, where it is #315. Hildebrand and Beckerlegge, eds., *Collection of Hymns*, 470.

Nine

Character of a Methodist

The spirituality that was developed by our Wesleyan founders was a lived process. Based on our inquiry, it would not be inappropriate to describe Methodist spirituality as a composite work—a patchwork quilt—formed from variegated and experience-laden pieces of fabric lovingly stitched to form a beautiful family heirloom. Rather, in this sense, our spirituality is a blend of our founders' Anglican interest in "forms," along with the more practical aims of the Puritans, fueled by careful study of the disciplines, aims of the Primitive Church, and great spiritual classics, with the spontaneous and "feeling" emphases of the Moravians mixed in.

Spiritual maturity, in the Methodist mode, is not something that comes upon a person suddenly and unbidden. Although there are moments of great depth and poignancy, ours is a formative spirituality—that is "practiced." Cultivating a spiritual life is more like learning an instrument, a sport, or a craft than it is like "falling in love," if by that we mean we expect it to come upon us unbidden and without warning. It is also clear that because of its composite character, Methodist spirituality has various points of entry and diverse emphases. This is very good, because living a Spirit-directed life is not a "one-size-fits-all" kind of thing; and recipes for it, however interesting or exotic they might be, will not work for everyone at every time. Rather, our founders would have us think of this undertaking as nothing less than building an ongoing relationship with the Living God. There are no shortcuts; rather, it is a journey that has no final destination this side of heaven. Indeed, because this is precisely the pilgrimage that forms and shapes us, the journey of life with God with its blessing and challenges; it is the journey *itself* that brings the desired results.

From their roots in the Church of England, the Wesleys learned to live a life punctuated by Morning and Evening Prayers, which were shaped by the *Book of Common Prayer* (*BCP*) or by using another "form." The *BCP* infused their lives and prayers with themes and images drawn from the Scriptures—particularly Psalms—the hymn-prayers of the Hebrew scriptures. For example, the Anglican emphasis on the Lord's Supper as "a means of grace" was embraced and extended into an entire lifestyle that the Wesleys handed to us as signifying the authentic "Character of a Methodist." This bequest encourages us to develop a sacramental worldview in which we learn to look for the invisible presence of God in and through the visible, tangible things all around us and through the challenges and blessings of our own lives.

This disciplined and life-oriented approach propelled the Wesleys to practice the five spiritual disciplines of "Primitive Christianity" (the pattern of the early church), which they esteemed to be "the means of grace," and whereby God in Christ could be encountered in converting and confirming ways. The same spiritual disciplines, such as the "works of piety" and "works of mercy," are rooted in a profound theology of gratitude and a robust understanding of Christian stewardship. They were an obvious outgrowth of the Wesleys' gospel of justification by faith, "faith which worketh by love" (Gal. 5:6). These disciplines were road tested and refined by the Wesleys own lifelong quest for renewed and transformed living, or in their own words, the "holiness, without which no one shall see the Lord" (Heb. 12:14).

In his famous tract by the same title, John Wesley described "The Character of a Methodist," from this same broad, life-embracing standpoint:[1]

A Methodist is one who has "the love of God shed abroad in his heart by the Holy Ghost given unto him;" one who "loves the Lord his God with all his heart, and with all his soul, and with all his mind, and with all his

---

1   Thomas Jackson, ed., *The Works of John Wesley, A.M.*, 14 vol., Vol. VIII, 341, "The Character of a Methodist," cf. https://www.umcmission.org/Find-Resources/John -Wesley-Sermons/The-Wesleys-and-Their-Times/The-Character-of-a-Methodist.

strength." God is the joy of his heart, and the desire of his soul; which is constantly crying out, "Whom have I in heaven but thee? and there is none upon earth that I desire beside thee! My God and my all! Thou art the strength of my heart, and my portion forever!"

John Wesley's tract, *The Character of a Methodist,* offers a pretty clear picture of what sort of inner life the practice of the "means of grace" could develop in a person. He explained that she/he:

Is happy in God
Lives a life shaped by hope and gratitude
"Prays without ceasing"; that is, lives a life permeated with prayer
"Exercises the love of God"
Designs his or her life to do the will of God
Keeps God's commandments from the heart
Desires to do good to all people—even the neighbor and the stranger.[2]

The characteristics John Wesley described as epitomizing Methodism were, in his words, "only the common fundamental principles of Christianity." He went on to describe Methodists as people who "vehemently refuse to be distinguished from other men, by any but the common principles of Christianity, the plain, old Christianity that I teach, renouncing and detesting all other marks of distinction."[3] What characterizes our own spirituality is to be found, not in our new or unique doctrines or distinctive practices, but in a particular quality of life that typifies the Wesleys' unique synthesis of attitudes and practices drawn from several important strands of the Christian tradition.

From their Puritan heritage the Wesleys learned to set goals and make spiritual resolutions in order to hold themselves accountable and to "stretch themselves out" as they deepened their relationship with God and, through grace, journeyed to become more Christ-like in their attitudes and actions. They learned to examine their conscience as a prelude to prayer and life, believing that self-knowledge leads one to a more objective and more accurate self-assessment, which is crucial both for effective prayer and for genuine spiritual growth. This added a profound sense of

---

2   Jackson, *Works of John Wesley,* Vol. VIII, 346.
3   Jackson, "The Character of a Methodist," 343.

stewardship and duty, which characterized their approach; therefore, the Wesleys sought to "redeem their time," because they viewed their time as both a finite resource and a wonderful gift from God. They lived all their lives with a deep sense of gratitude and sense of responsibility to use all things well, recognizing that all they were and all they had came to them directly from God's bountiful generosity.

The Moravian emphasis upon justification by faith as "a faith you could feel," delivered the Wesleys from a frustrating life of religious duties by which they found themselves preoccupied with trying to earn God's approval. They learned the experiential difference between living the obligatory "faith of a servant," as opposed to embracing liberating and joy-filled "faith of a son"—living as a warmly accepted child of God. This life lesson left them with a deep awareness of the importance of an inner and experiential sense of God's acceptance, which they termed "the witness of the Spirit."

The Moravian use of small groups for spiritual formation merged well with what the Wesleys had learned from their Anglican and Puritan pre-decessors. Consequently John and Charles extended it into a full-orbed pattern and plan for equipping women and men to become and to live as what they understood as "the Primitive Church." The Moravians also reminded the Wesleys of the spiritual and devotional power of popular hymnody. It was a lesson they first learned in childhood, by singing hymns with Susanna in the kitchen, and then it was strongly reinforced firsthand by watching a small band of Moravians prayerfully and courageously sing-ing their way through a howling Atlantic gale. Wesleyan hymnody would become the background music and sound track of Methodist spiritual-ity as well as being a strong bulwark against the horrific storms and soul-straining events in individual lives.

From this rich legacy, we modern Methodists have inherited a con-cern for spiritual disciplines: prayer, Scripture study, the Lord's Supper, fasting, Christian conferencing or close spiritual fellowship, and works of piety and mercy. They saw them as channels and means whereby we can encounter our gracious God. Of these disciplines, however, prayer (personal, family, and corporate) is the foundation and energizer of the others. As a "means of grace," prayer is not simply going to God with a laundry list of needs, wants, and petitions. But, in the larger sense, prayer becomes a window through which we can "see" and experience God and God's grace, any place, any time. At the core, prayer is meeting God in Christ, and it is in a profound sense a means of grace; because Christ is the only means, and through faith-filled encounters with Christ, we meet God and experience God's love, kindness, joy, acceptance, and forgiveness for ourselves.

Those of us who seek to pray like the Wesleys should think of prayer as being inspired and shaped primarily by the language and insights of the Bible but also other resources from Christian tradition. Yet, prayer should also be a spontaneous act of "pouring our hearts out before God." As we prepare to pray, we should be taking stock of our lives—our "inward and outward state"—by looking at our aims and attitudes through an examination of conscience.

For Methodists, prayer takes three forms: private, family, and corporate. John Wesley stressed the critical importance of private prayer, or personal devotions, particularly for his ministers, whom he persistently asked: "Do you use all of these?" Those who failed to develop a significant prayer life or to pray regularly Wesley consigned to the "wilderness state," that is devoid of good and godly things.

After meditation and examination of one's conscience as a prelude to prayer, the Wesleys urge us to consider several specific aspects of prayer. John Wesley delineated four (though sometimes three) parts to formal prayer: "deprecation" (preparing to confession of praise and sorrow), petition, intercession, and thanksgiving. Since our entire life is based upon "constant communion" with God, we must develop the ability to "pray without ceasing." This, wrote, John Wesley, is to be the language of our heart: "'Thou brightness of eternal glory, unto Thee is my heart, though without a voice, my silence speaketh onto Thee.' And this is true prayer, and this alone. But [the Methodist's] heart is ever lifted up to God, at all times and in all places. . . . God is in all his thoughts; he walks with God continually, having the loving eye of his mind still fixed on Him, and everywhere seeing Him that is invisible."[4]

We witness to our faith, which is invigorated through our "works of piety" and "works of mercy." This is a life of "constant communion" with God; one that is shaped by gratitude, joy, and a willingness to be a servant. Thus, John Wesley urged the early Methodists, as he would urge us today,

---

4   Jackson, ed., 343.

to "intermix piety and justice" and join the "desires of our hearts with the labor of our hands." Prayer, then, can continue throughout all of our works, since "prayer continues the desire of the heart, though the understanding be employed on outward things." Hence, in the Wesleys' view, all the tasks Christians undertake, they should do in prayer.

If one were to try to condense prayer in the Wesleyan mode to a list of essential characteristics, the following would certainly need to be on that list. Hopefully these aspects can become a source of reflection and spiritual growth for each of us:

1. Prayer is a means of grace in which we have the opportunity to encounter God through Jesus Christ, under the guidance of the Holy Spirit.
2. We can effectively pray using Scripture, hymns, and devotional aids, as well as our own words.
3. Prayer has several basic parts, including confession, petition, intercession, and thanksgiving.
4. Effective prayer can also be spontaneous and Spirit-directed; the Holy Spirit urges us to pour out our souls before God; and when we cannot find words, the Spirit intercedes for us.
5. Prayer is fundamentally *about God,* God who wants to be in relationship with us, and through God's loving-kindness and gracious bounty gives us clear reason for petition, thanksgiving, and praise.
6. Prayer is also *about us,* about our "inward and outward states"; hence, taking stock of ourselves through a frank examination of conscience is necessary.
7. Prayer is more about who we *are* and who we're *called to be* as children of God. It is less about what particular things we are praying for.
8. Prayer is both private and public, and while it takes diverse forms, consistent personal prayer provides the basis of everything else.
9. Private prayer is critically important for our own spiritual health and well-being; and if we neglect prayer, we walk away from our relationship with God and will easily fall into "the wilderness state."
10. Prayer is fundamentally a "constant communion with God," which joins "the desires of our hearts with the works of our hands."

Hence, "all that a Christian does . . . is prayer, when it is done in simplicity, according to the order of God." Or as one of Charles's hymns urges:

> Let us go forth, 'tis God commands;
> Let us make haste away,
> Offer to Christ our hearts and hands,
> We work for Christ today.[5]

---

5   William Osborn, *The Poetical Works of John and Charles Wesley*, 13 vols. (London: Methodist Conference, 1872), Vol. II, 17.

Appendix A

The Methodist Daily Office: A Collection of Forms of Prayer for Every Day of the Week by John Wesley (1733)[1]

Whoever follows the direction of our excellent Church in the interpretation of the Holy Scriptures by keeping close to that sense of them which the catholic fathers and ancient bishops have delivered to succeeding generations will easily see that the whole system of Christian duty is reducible to these five heads:

First, the renouncing ourselves. "If any man will come after me, let him *renounce* himself . . . and follow me [Mt. 16:24]." This implies, first a thorough conviction that we are not our own, that we are not the proprietors of ourselves or anything we enjoy, that we have no right to dispose of our goods, bodies, souls, or any of the actions or passions of them. Secondly, a solemn resolution to act suitably to this conviction: not to live to ourselves, nor to suffer [e.g. "allow"] our own will to be any principle of action to us.

Secondly, such a renunciation of ourselves naturally leads to the *devoting of ourselves to God.* As this implies, first, a thorough conviction that we are God's; that He is the proprietor of all we are and all we have; and that not only by right of creation but of purchase; for He died for all, and therefore "died for all, that they which live should not henceforth live unto themselves, but unto Him that died for them." Secondly, a solemn resolution to act suitably to this conviction: to live

1   Thomas Jackson, ed., *Works of John Wesley, A.M.*, 14 vol. (London: Wesleyan Conference, 1872), Vol. XI, 271–72, "The Preface," with omissions, and emphasis added.

unto God; to render unto God the things which are God's, even all we are and all we have; to glorify Him in our bodies and in our spirits with all the powers and all the strength of each; and to make His will our sole principle of action.

Thirdly, self-denial is the immediate consequence of this. For whosoever has determined to live no longer to the desires of men but to the will of God will soon find that he cannot be true to his purpose without denying himself and taking up his cross daily. He will daily feel some desire which this one principle of action; the will of God, does not require him to indulge. In this therefore, he must either deny himself or so far deny the faith. He will daily meet with some means of drawing nearer to God which are pleasing to flesh and blood. In this therefore, he must either take up his cross or so far renounce his Master.

Fourthly, by a constant exercise of self-denial, the true follower of Christ continually advances in mortification. He is more and more dead to the world and the things of the world, till at length he can say, with that perfect disciple of his Lord, Marquis de Renty, "I desire nothing but God," or with Paul, "I am crucified unto the world; I am dead with Christ; I live not, but Christ liveth in me."

Fifthly, Christ liveth in me. This is the fulfilling of the law, the last stage of Christian holiness; this maketh the man of God perfect. He that being dead to the world is alive to God; the desire of whose soul is unto His name; who has given Him his whole heart; who delights in Him and in nothing else but what tends to Him; who for His sake burns with love to all mankind; who neither thinks, speaks, nor acts but to fulfill His will, is on the last round of the ladder to heaven; grace hath had its full work upon his soul; the next step he takes is into glory.

May the God of glory give unto us who have not already attained this, neither are already perfect, to do this one thing, forgetting those things which are behind and reaching forth unto those things which are before, to press toward the mark for the prize of our high calling in Christ Jesus.

May He so enlighten our eyes that we may reckon all things but loss for the excellency of the knowledge of Christ Jesus our Lord, and so stablish our hearts that we may rejoice to suffer the loss of all things and count them but dung that we may win Christ.

For Sunday Morning[2]

Almighty God, Father of all mercies, I, thy unworthy servant, desire to present myself, with all humility, before Thee to offer my morning sacrifices of love and thanksgiving.

Glory be to Thee, O most adorable Father, who after Thou hadst finished the work of creation, entered into Thy eternal rest. Glory be to Thee, O holy Jesus, who having through sacrifice for the sins of the whole world, didst rise again the third day from the dead, and hadst All power given Thee both in heaven and on earth.

Glory be to Thee, O blessed Spirit, who, proceeding from the Father and the Son, didst come down in fiery tongues on the Apostles on the first day of the week, and didst enable them to preach the glad tidings of salvation to a sinful world, and hast ever since been moving on the faces of men's souls, as Thou did once on the face of the great deep, bringing them out of that dark chaos in which they were involved.

Glory be to Thee, O holy, undivided Trinity, for jointly concurring in the great work of our redemption and restoring us again to the glorious liberty of the sons of God. Glory be to Thee, who in compassion to human weakness, hast appointed a solemn day for the remembrance of thy inestimable benefits. O let me ever esteem it my privilege and happiness to have a day set apart for the concerns of my soul, a day free from distractions, disengaged from the world, wherein I have nothing to do but to praise and love Thee. O let it ever be to me a day sacred to divine love, a day of heavenly rest and refreshment.

Let Thy Holy Spirit, who, on the first day of the week, descended in miraculous gifts on thy Apostles, descend on me, thy unworthy servant, that I may be always "in the spirit of the Lord's day." Let his blessed inspiration prevent and assist me in all the duties of this Thy sacred day, that my wandering thoughts may all be fixed on Thee, my tumultuous affections composed, and my flat and cold desires quickened into fervent longings and thirstings after Thee. O let me join in the prayers and praises of Thy Church with ardent and heavenly affection, hear Thy word with earnest attention and a fixed resolve to obey it. And when I approach Thy altar,

---

2   Jackson, ed., 203–37. "A Collection of Forms of Prayer," capitalization and spelling have been modified.

pour into my heart humility, faith, hope, love, and all those holy disposi-tions which become the solemn remembrance of a crucified Savior. Let me employ this whole day to the ends for which it was ordained, in works of necessity and mercy, in prayer, praise, and meditation; and "let the words of my mouth, and the meditation of my heart be always accept-able in Thy sight."

I know, O Lord, that Thou hast commanded me, and therefore it is my duty, to love Thee with all my heart, and with all my strength. I know Thou are infinitely holy and overflowing in all perfection; and therefore it is my duty so to love Thee.

I know Thou art the end for which I was created, and that I can expect no happiness but in Thee.

I know that in love to me, being lost in sin, Thou didst send Thy only Son, and that He, being the Lord of glory, did humble himself to the death upon the cross, that I might be raised in glory.

I know thou has provided me with all necessary helps for carrying me through this life to that eternal glory, and this out of the excess of thy pure mercy to me, unworthy of all mercies.

I know Thou hast promised to be Thyself my "exceeding great reward"; though it is Thou alone who Thyself "workest in me, both to will and to do Thy good pleasure."

Upon these, and many other titles, I confess it is my duty to love Thee, my God with all my heart. Give Thy strength unto Thy servant, that Thy love may fill my heart, and be the motive of all the use I make of my under-standing, my affections, my senses, my health, my time, and whatever other talents I have received from Thee. Let this, O God, rule my heart with-out a rival; let it dispose all my thoughts, words, and works; and thus only can I fulfill my duty and thy command, of loving thee "with all my heart, and mind, and soul, and strength."

O Thou infinite Goodness, confirm Thy past mercies to me, by enabling me, for what remains of my life, to be more faithful than I have hitherto been to this Thy great command. For the time I have yet to sojourn upon earth, O let me fulfill this great duty. Permit me not to be in any delusion here; let me not trust in words, nor sighs, or tears, but love Thee even as Thou hast commanded. Let me feel, and then I shall know, what it is to love Thee with all my heart.

O merciful God, whatsoever Thou deniest me, deny me not this love. Save me from the idolatry of "loving the world, or any of the things of the world." Let me never love any creature, but for thy sake, and in subordination to Thy love. Take Thou the full possession of my heart; raise there Thy throne, and command there as Thou does in heaven. Being created by Thee, let me live to Thee; being created for Thee, let me ever act for Thy glory; being redeemed by Thee, let me render unto Thee what is Thine, and let my spirit ever cleave to Thee alone.

Let the prayers and sacrifices of Thy holy Church, offered unto Thee this day, be graciously accepted. "Clothe Thy priests with righteousness and pardon all Thy people who are not prepared according to the preparation of the sanctuary." Prosper all those who are sincerely engaged in propagating or promoting Thy faith and love [particular names may be added here]; O Give thy Son of the Heathen for all His inheritance, and the utmost part of the earth for His possession; that from the rising up of the sun unto the going down of the same, Thy name may be great among those whom Thou hast set over us in Church and State, in our several stations, to serve Thee in all holiness, and to "know the love of Christ which passeth knowledge."

Continue to us the means of grace, and grant we may never provoke Thee, by our improvement, to deprive us of them. Pour down Thy blessing upon our Universities, that they may ever promote true religion and sound learning. Show mercy, O Lord, to my father and mother, my brothers and sisters, to all my friends [here particular names may be added] relations, and enemies and to all that are in affliction. Let Thy fatherly hand be over them, and Thy Holy Spirit ever with them; that, submitting themselves entirely to Thy will, and directing all their thoughts, words, and works to Thy glory, they, and those that are already dead in the Lord, may at length enjoy Thee, in the glories of Thy kingdom, through Jesus Christ our Lord, Who liveth and reigneth with Thee and the Holy Ghost, one God, blessed forever.

Sunday Evening

General Questions which a Serious Christian May Propose to Himself before He Begins His Evening Devotions

1. With what degree of attention and fervor did I use my morning prayers, public or private?

2. Have I done anything without a present, or at least a previous, perception of its direct or remote tendency to the glory of God?
3. Did I in the morning consider what particular virtue I was to exercise, and what business I had to do in the day?
4. Have I been zealous to undertake, and active in doing, what good I could?
5. Have I interested myself any farther in the affairs of others than charity required?
6. Have I, before I visited or was visited, considered how I might thereby give or receive improvement?
7. Have I mentioned any failing or fault of any man, when it was not necessary for the good of another?
8. Have I unnecessarily grieved anyone by word or deed?
9. Have I before or in every action considered how it might be a means of improving in the virtue of the day?

Particular Questions to the Love of God

1. Have I set apart of this day to think upon His perfections and mercies?
2. Have I labored to make this day a day of heavenly rest, sacred to divine love?
3. Have I employed those parts of it in works necessity and mercy, which were not employed in Prayer, reading and meditation?

O my Father, my God! I am in Thy hand; and may I rejoice above all things in being so. Do with me what seemed good in Thy sight, not only let me love Thee with all my mind, soul and strength.

I magnify Thee for granting me to be born in Thy Church, and of religious parents; for washing me in Thy baptism, and instructing Thy baptism; for instructing me in Thy doctrine of truth and holiness; for sustaining me by Thy gracious providence, and guiding me by thy ever blessed Spirit; for admitting me, with the rest of my Christian brethren, to wait on Thee at Thy public worship; and so often feeding my soul with Thy most precious body and blood, those pledges of thy love, and sure conveyance of strength and comfort. O be gracious unto all of us, whom Thou hast this day (or at any time) admitted to thy holy table. Strengthen our hearts in

Thy ways against all our temptations, and make us, "more than conquerors" in Thy love.

O my Father, my God, deliver me, I beseech Thee, from all violent passions: I know how greatly obstructive these are both of the knowledge and love of Thee. O let none of them find a way into my heart, but let me ever possess my soul in meekness. O my God, I desire to fear them more than death; let me not serve these cruel tyrants, but to Thou reign in my breast; let me be ever Thy servant and love Thee with all my heart.

Deliver me, O God, from too intense an application to even necessary business. I know how this dissipates my thoughts from one end of all my business and impairs that lively perception I would even retain of Thee standing at my right hand. I know the narrowness of my heart, and that an eager attention to earthly things leave it no room for the things of heaven. O teach me to go through all my employments with so truly disengaged a heart, that I may still see Thee in all things, and see Thee therein as continually looking upon me, and searching my reins; and that I may never impair that liberty of spirit which is necessary for the love of Thee.

Deliver me, O God, from a slothful mind, from all lukewarmness and all dejection of spirit. I know these cannot but deaden my love to Thee; mercifully free my heart from them, and give me a lively, zealous, cheerful spirit; that I may vigorously perform whatever Thou commandest, thankfully suffer whatever Thou choosest for me, and be ever ardent to obey in all things Thy holy love.

Deliver me, O God, from all idolatrous love of any creature. I know infinite numbers have been lost to thee by loving those creatures for their own sake, which Thou permittest, nay even commandest, to love subordinately to Thee. Preserve me, I beseech Thee, from all such blind affection; be thou a guard to all my desires, that they fix on no creature any farther than the love of it tends to build me up in the love of Thee. Thou requires me to love Thee with all my heart: Undertake for me, I beseech Thee, and be Thou my security, that I may never open my heart to anything, but out of love to Thee.

Above all, deliver me, O my God, from all idolatrous self-love. I know, O god, (blessed by Thy infinite mercy for giving me this knowledge) that this is the root of all evil. I know Thou madest me, not to do my own will, but Thine. I know, the very corruption of the Devil is, the having a will contrary to Thine. O be Thou my helper against this most dangerous of all idols, that I may both discern all its subtleties, and withstand all its force. O Thou who has commanded me to renounce myself, give me strength, and I will obey Thy command. My choice and my desire is, to love myself as all other creatures, in and for Thee. O let Thy almighty arm so stablish, strengthen, and settle me, that Thou mayest ever be the ground and pillar of all my love.

O my God, let Thy glorious name be duly honored and loved by all the creatures which Thou has made. Let Thy infinite goodness and greatness be ever adored by all angels and men. May Thy Church, the catholic seminary of divine love, be protected from all the powers of darkness. O vouchsafe to all who call themselves by Thy name one short glimpse of Thy goodness. May they once taste and see how gracious Thou art, that all things else may be tasteless to them; that their desires may be always flying up towards Thee, that they may render Thee love, and praise, and obedience, pure and cheerful, constant and zealous, universal and uniform, like that the holy angels render Thee in heaven.

Send forth Thy blessed Spirit into the midst of these sinful nations, and make us a holy people: stir up the heart of our Sovereign, of the Royal Family, of the clergy, the nobility and all of whom Thou hast set over us, that they may be happy instruments in Thy hand of promoting this good work. Be gracious to the Universities, to the Gentry and Commons of this land: and comfort all that are in affliction; let the trial of their faith work patience in them, and perfect them in hope and love.

Bless my father and etc., my friends and relations, and all that belong to this family; all that have been instrumental to my good, by their assistance, advice, example, or writing; and all that do not pray for themselves.

Change the hearts of mine enemies, and give me grace to forgive them, even as Thou for Christ's sake forgives us.

O Thou Shepherd of Israel, vouchsafe to receive me this night and ever into Thy protection; accept my poor services, and pardon the sinfulness of these and all my holy duties. O let it be Thy good pleasure shortly to put a period to sin and misery, to infirmity and death, to complete the number of Thine elect, and to hasten Thy kingdom; that we, and all that wait for Thy salvation, may eternally love and praise Thee, O God the Father, God the Son, and God the Holy Ghost, throughout all ages, world without end.

"Our Father and etc."

Monday Morning

General Questions, which May Be Used Every Morning

Did I think of God first and last?

Have I examined myself how I behaved since last night's retirement?

Am I resolved to do all the good I can this day, and to be diligent in the business of my calling?

O God, who art the giver of all good gifts, I Thy unworthy servant entirely desire to praise Thy name for all the expressions of Thy bounty towards me. Blessed by Thy love Thy Son to die for our sins, for the means of grace, and for the hope of glory. Blessed by Thy love for all the temporal benefits which Thou as with a liberal hand poured out upon me; for my health, and strength, food and raiment, and all other necessities with which Thou hast provided Thy sinful servant. I also bless Thee that, after all my refusals of Thy grace, Thou still hast patience with me, hast preserved me this night and given me yet another day to renew and perfect my repentance. Pardon, good Lord, all my former sins, and make me every day more and more zealous and diligent to improve every opportunity of building up my soul in Thy faith, and love, and obedience. Make Thyself always present to my mind, and let Thy love fill and rule my soul, in all those places, and companies, and employments to which Thou callest me this day. In all my passage through this world, suffer not my heart to be set upon it; but always fix my single eye and my undivided affections on "the prize of my high calling." This one thing let me do; let me so press toward this, as to make all things minister unto it; and be careful so to use them, as thereby to fit my soul for that pure bliss which Thou hast prepared for those that love Thee.

O Thou, Who art good and doest good, who extendest Thy loving-kindness to all mankind, the work of Thine hands, Thine image, capable of knowing and loving Thee eternally: Suffer me to exclude none, O Lord, from my charity, who are the objects of Thy mercy; but let me treat all my neighbors with that tender love which is due to Thy servants and to Thy children. Thou hast required this mark of my love to Thee, O let no temptation expose me to ingratitude, or make me forfeit Thy lovingkindness, which is better than life itself. But grant that I may assist all my brethren with my prayers, which I cannot reach them with actual services. Make me zealous to embrace all occasions that may administer to their happiness, by assisting the needy, protecting the oppressed, instructing the ignorant, confirming the wavering, exhorting the good, and reproving the wicked. Let me look up[on] the failings of my neighbor as if they were my own; that I may be grieved form them, that I may never reveal them but when charity requires, and then with tenderness and compassion. Let Thy love to me, O blessed Savior, be the pattern of my love to him. Thou thoughtest nothing too dear to part with, to rescue me from eternal misery: O let me think nothing too dear to part with to set forward the everlasting good of my fellow Christians. They are members of Thy body; therefore I will cherish them. Thou hast redeemed them with an inestimable price; assisted by Thy Holy Spirit, therefore, I will endeavor to recover them from a state of destruction; that thus adoring Thy holy gospel, by doing good according to my power, I may at last be received into the endearments of Thy eternal love, and sing everlasting praise upon the Lamb that was slain and sitteth on the throne forever.

Extend, I humbly beseech Thee, Thy mercy to all men, and let them become Thy faithful servants. Let all Christians live up to the holy religion they profess; especially these sinful nations. Be entreated for us, good Lord; be glorified by our reformation, and not by our destruction. "Turn Thou us, and so shall we be turned." O be favorable to Thy people; give us grace to put a period to our punishment. Defend our Church from schism, heresy, and sacrilege, and the King and Deacons, with apostolic graces, exemplary lives, and sound doctrine. Grant to the Council wisdom from above, to all Magistrates integrity and zeal, to the Universities quietness and industry, and to the Gentry and Commons pious and peaceable hearts.

Monday Evening

Particular Questions Relating to the Love of Our Neighbor

1. Have I thought anything but my conscience too dear to part with, to please or serve my neighbor?
2. Have I rejoiced or grieved with him?
3. Have I received his infirmities with pity, and not with anger?

4. Have I contradicted any one, either where I had no good end in view, or where there was no probability of convincing?
5. Have I let him I thought in the wrong (in a trifle) have the last word?

Most good and glorious Lord God, I desire to prostrate myself before Thy divine Majesty, under a deep sense of my unworthiness; and with sorrow, and shame, and confusion of face, to confess I have, by my manifold transgressions, deserved thy severest visitations. "Father I have sinned against heaven and am no more worthy to be called thy son"; O let thy paternal bowels yearn upon me, and for Jesus Christ's sake graciously receive me. Accept my imperfect repentance, and send Thy Spirit of adoption into my heart, that I may again be saved by Thee, call Thee Father, and share in the blessings of Thy children.

Adored by Thy goodness for all the benefits Thou has already from time to time bestowed on me; for the good things of this life, and the hope of eternal happiness. Particularly, I offer to Thee my humblest thanks for Thy preservation of me this day. If I have escaped any sin, it is the effect of Thy restraining grace; if I have avoided any danger, it was Thy hand that directed me. To Thy holy name be ascribed the honor and glory. O let the sense of all Thy blessedness have this effect upon me, —to make me daily more diligent in devoting myself, all I am, and all I have, to Thy glory.

O my God, fill my soul with so entire a love of Thee, that I may love nothing but for Thy sake and in subordination to Thy love. Give me grace to study Thy knowledge daily, that the more I know Thee, the more I may love Thee. Create me a zealous obedience to all Thy commandments, a cheerful patience under Thy chastisements, and a thankful resignation to all Thy disposals. My I ever have awful thoughts of Thee; never mention Thy venerable name, unless on just, solemn, and devout occasions; nor even then without acts of adoration. O let it be the one business of my life to glorify Thee, by every thought of my heart, by every word of my tongue, by every work of my hand; by professing Thy truth, even to the death if it should please Thee to call me to it, and by engaging all men, as far as in lies, to glorify and love Thee.

Let Thy unwearied and tender love to me, make my love unwearied and tender to my neighbors, zealous to pray for, and to procure and promote, his health and safety, ease and happiness; and active to comfort, succor, and relieve all whom Thy love and their own necessities recommended to my charity. Make me peaceful and reconcilable; easy to forgive, and glad to return good for evil. Make me like Thyself, all kindness and benignity. And, O Thou lover of my soul, raise in me a compassionate zeal to save the life, the eternal life, of souls; and by affectionate and seasonable advice, exhortations, and reproof, to reclaim the wicked, and win them to Thy love.

Be pleased, O Lord, to take me, with my father and mother, brethren and sisters, my friends and my relations, and my enemies, into Thy almighty protection this night. Refresh me with such comfortable rest that I may rise more fit for Thy service. Let me lie down with holy thoughts of Thee; and when I awake let me be still present with Thee.

Show mercy to the whole world, O Father of all; let the gospel of the Son run and be glorified throughout all the earth. Let it be made known to all in infidels and obeyed by all Christians. Be merciful to this Church, and nation; give unto Thy Bishops a discerning spirit, that they may make choice of fit persons to serve in Thy sacred ministry; and enable all who are ordained to any holy function, diligently to feed the flocks committed to their charge, instructing them in saving knowledge, guiding them by their examples, praying for and blessing them, exercising spiritual disciples in Thy Church, and duly administering Thy holy sacraments. Multiply Thy blessings on our Sovereign, on the Royal Family and on the Nobles, Magistrates, Gentry, and Commons of this land; that they may all, according to the several talents they have received, be faithful instruments of Thy glory. Give to our Schools and Universities, zeal and prudence, and holiness. Visit in mercy all the children of affliction, [name s here] relieve their necessities, lighten their burdens; give them a cheerful submission to Thy gracious will, and at length bring them and us, with those that already rest from their labors, into the joy of our Lord; to whom with Thee, O Father, and Thee O Holy Ghost, be all praise, now and forever.

Tuesday Morning

O Eternal and merciful Father, I give Thee humble thanks (increase my thankfulness, I beseech Thee) for all the blessings, spiritual and temporal, which, in the riches of Thy mercy, Thou hast poured down upon me. Lord, let me not live but to love Thee, and to glorify Thy name. Particularly, I give Thee most unfeigned thanks for preserving me from my birth to this moment, and for bringing me safe to the beginning of this day in which, and in all the days of my life, I beseech Thee that all my thoughts, words, and works, may tend to Thy glory. Heal, O Father of mercies, all my infirmities [mention some], strengthen me against all my follies; forgive me all my sins [name some], and let them not cry louder in Thine ears for vengeance, than my prayers for mercy and forgiveness.

O blessed Lord, enable me to fulfill Thy commands and command what Thou wilt. O Thou Savior of all that trust in Thee, do with me what seemeth best in Thine own eyes; only give me the mind which was in Thee; let me learn of Thee to be meek and lowly. Pour into me the whole spirit of humility; fill, I beseech Thee, every part of my soul with it, and make it the constant, ruling habit of my mind, that all my other tempers may arise from it; that I may have no thoughts, no designs, but such as are the true fruit of a lowly spirit. Grant that I may think of myself as I ought to think, that I may "know myself even as I am known." Here in may I exercise myself continually, when I lie down and when I rise up, that I may always appear poor, and little and mean and base, and vile in mine own eyes. O convince me that "I have neither learned wisdom, nor have the knowledge of the holy." Give me a lively sense that I am nothing, that I have nothing, and that I can do nothing. Enable me to feel that I am all ignorance and error, weakness and uncleanness, sin and misery; that I am not worthy of the air I breathe, the earth I tread upon, or the sun that shines upon me. And let me be fully content when all other men think of me as I do of myself. O save me from either desiring or seeking the honor that cometh of men. Convince me that the words of praise, "when smoother than oil," then especially "are very swords." Give me to dread them more than the "poison of asps, or any pestilence that walketh in darkness." And when these cords of pride, these snares of death, do overtake me, suffer me not to take any pleasure in them, but enable me instantly to flee unto Thee, O Lord, and to complain unto my God. Let all my bones cry out, "Thou are worth to be praised; so shall I be safe from mine enemies."

Bless, O gracious Father, all the nations, whom Thou hast placed upon the earth, with the knowledge of Thee, the only true God: but especially bless Thy holy catholic [universal] church and fill it with truth and grace; where it is corrupt, purge it; where it is in error, rectify it; where it is right, confirm it; where it is divided and rent asunder, heal the breaches thereof, O Thou Holy One of Israel. Replenish all whom Thou hast called to any office therein with truth of doctrine and innocency of life. Let their prayers be as precious incense in Thy sight, that their cries and tears for the city of their God may not be in vain.

O Lord, hear the King in the day of his trouble; let Thy name, O God, defend him. Grant him his heart's desire and fulfill all his mind. Set his heart firm upon Thee, and upon other things only as they are in and for Thee. O defend him and his royal relations from Thy holy heaven, even with the saving strength of Thy right hand.

Have mercy upon this Kingdom and forgive the sins of this people; turn Thee unto us and cause Thy face to shine on our desolations. Inspire the Nobles and Magistrates with prudent zeal, the Gentry and Commons with humble loyalty. Pour down Thy blessings on all seminaries of true religion and learning, that they may remember and answer the end of their institutions. Comfort all the sons and daughters or affliction, especially those who suffer for righteousness' sake. Bless my father and mother, my brethren and sisters, my friends and relations, and all that belong to this family. Forgive all who are mine enemies, and so reconcile them to me and Thyself, that we all, together with those now asleep in Thee. May awake to life everlasting, through Thy merits and intercession, O blessed Jesus; to Whom, with the Father and the Holy Ghost, be ascribed, by all creatures, "all honor and might, and wisdom, and glory, and blessing."

Tuesday Evening

Particular Questions Relating to Humility

1. Have I labored to conform all my thoughts, words, and actions to these fundamental maxims; "I am nothing. I have nothing. I can do nothing"?
2. Have I set apart some time this day to think upon my infirmities, follies, and sins?
3. Have I ascribed to myself any part of any good which God did by my hand?
4. Have I said or done anything with a view to the praise of men?
5. Have I desired the praise of men?
6. Have I taken pleasure in it?
7. Have I commended myself, or others, to their faces unless for God's sake, and then with fear and trembling?

8. Have I despised any one's advice?
9. Have I, when I thought so, said, "I am in the wrong"?
10. Have I received contempt for things indifferent, with meekness? For doing my duty, with joy?
11. Have I omitted justifying myself where the glory of God was not concerned? Have I submitted to be thought in the wrong?
12. Have I, when condemned, First prayed God it might not discourage or puff me up; Secondly, that it might not be imputed to the condemner; Thirdly, that it might heal my pride?
13. Have I, without some particular good in view, mentioned the contempt I had met with?

I desire to offer unto Thee, O Lord, my evening sacrifice—the sacrifice of a contrite spirit. "Have mercy upon me, O God, after Thy great goodness, and after the multitude of Thy mercies do away mine offences." Let Thy unspeakable mercy free me from the sins I have committed and deliver me from the punishment I have deserved [name them]. O save me from every work of darkness and cleanse me "from all filthiness of flesh and spirit," that, for the time to come, I may, with a pure heart and mind, follow Thee, the only true God.

O Lamb of God, Who, both by Thy example and precept, didst instruct us to be meek and humble, give me grace throughout my whole life, in every thought, and word, and work, to imitate Thy meekness and humility, O mortify in me the whole body of pride; grant me to feel that I am nothing and have nothing, and that I deserve nothing but shame and contempt, but misery and punishment. Grant, O Lord, that I may look for nothing, claim nothing; and that I may go through all the scenes of life, not seeking my own glory, but looking wholly unto Thee, and acting wholly for Thee. Let me never speak any word that may tend to my own praise, unless the good of my neighbor require it; and even then let me beware, lest, to heal another, I wound my own soul. Let my ears and my heart be ever shut to the praise that cometh of men and let me "refuse to hear the voice of the charmer, charm he never so sweetly." Give me a dread of applause, in whatsoever form, and from whatsoever tongue, it cometh. I know that "many stronger men have been slain by it," and that it "leadeth to the chambers of death." O deliver my souls for this snare of hell; neither let me spread it for the feet of others. Whosoever perish thereby, be their blood upon their own head, and let my hand be upon them.

O Thou Giver of every good and perfect gift, if at any time Thou pleases to work by my hand, teach me to discern what is my own from what is another's, and to render unto Thee the things that are Thine. As all the good that is done on earth Thou doest it Thyself, let me ever return to Thee all the glory. Let me, as a pure crystal, transmit all the light Thou pourest upon me; but never claim as my own what is Thy sole property.

O Thou Who were despised and rejected of men, when I am slighted by my friends, disdained by my superiors, overborne or ridiculed by my equals, or contemptuously treated by my inferiors, let me cry out with Thy holy martyr [Ignatius], "It is now that I begin to be a disciple of Christ." Then let me thankfully accept, and faithfully use, the happy occasion of improving in Thy meek and lowly spirit. If for Thy sake "men cast out my name as evil," let me "rejoice and be exceedingly glad." If for my own infirmities, yet let me acknowledge Thy goodness, in giving me this medicine to heal my pride and vanity and beg Thy mercy for those physicians of my soul by whose hands it is administered to me.

"Make me to remember Thee on my bed, and think upon Thee when I am walking," Thou hast preserved me from all dangers of the day past; Thou hast been my support from my youth up until now; "under the shadow of Thy wings" let me pass this night in comfort and peace.

O Thou Creator and Preserver of all mankind, have mercy upon all conditions of men; purge Thy holy catholic Church from all heresy, schism, and superstition. Bless our Sovereign in his person, in his actions, in his relations and in his people. May it please Thee, "to endue his Council and all the Nobility, with grace, wisdom, and understanding;" the Magistrates, with equity, courage, and prudence; the Gentry, with industry and temperance; and all the Commons of this land, with increase of grace, and a holy humble, thankful spirit.

O pour upon our whole Church, and especially upon the Clergy thereof, the continual dew of Thy blessings. Grant to our Universities peace and piety; and to all that labor under affliction, constant patience and timely deliverance. Bless all my kindred, especially my father and mother, my brothers and sisters, and all my friends, and benefactors [names]. Turn the hearts of my enemies; [names] forgive them and me all our sins, and grant that we, and all the members of thy holy Church, may find mercy in the dreadful day of judgment, through the mediation and satisfaction of Thy blessed Son Jesus Christ; to Whom, with Thee and the Holy Ghost the Comforter, be all honor, praise, and thanksgiving, in all the Churches of the saints forever.

Wednesday Morning

O Thou Who dwellest in the light which no man can approach, in Whose presence there is no night, in the light of Whose countenance there is perpetual day; I, thy sinful servant, whom Thou has preserved this night, who live by Thy power this day, bless and glorify Thee for the defense of Thy almighty providence, [name some] and humbly pray Thee, that this, and all my days, may be wholly devoted to Thy service. Send Thy Holy Spirit to be the Guide of all my ways, and the sanctifier of my soul and body. Save, defend, and build me up in Thy fear and love; give unto me the light of Thy countenance, peace from heaven, and the salvation of my soul in the day of the Lord Jesus.

O Thou Who art "the Way, the Truth, and the Life," Thou hast said no man can follow Thee, unless he renounces himself. I know, O Savior, that Thou hast laid nothing upon us but what the design of Thy love made necessary for us. Thou sawest our disease, our idolatrous self-love, whereby we fell away from God, to be as gods ourselves, to please ourselves, and to do our own will. Lo, I come! May I ever renounce my own and do Thy blessed will in all things!

I know, O God, Thou didst empty Thyself of Thy eternal glory, and tookest upon Thee, "the form of a servant." Thou who madest all men to serve and please Thee, didst not please Thyself, but wast the servant of all. Thou, O Lord of the hosts of heaven and earth, didst yield Thy cheeks to be smitten, Thy back to be scourged, and Thy hands and feet to be nailed to an accursed tree. Thus didst Thou, our great Master, renounce Thyself; and can we think much of renouncing our vile selves? My Lord and my God, let me not presume to be above my Master! Let it be the one desire of my heart, to be as my Master; to do not my own will, but the will of Him that sent me.

O Thou Whose whole life did cry aloud, "Father, not mine but Thy will be done," give me grace to walk after Thy pattern; to tread in Thy steps. Give me grace to "take up my cross daily," to inure myself to bear hardship.

Let me exercise myself unto godliness betimes, before the rains descend and the floods beat upon me. Let me now practice what is not pleasing to flesh and blood, what is not agreeable to my senses, appetites, and passions, that I may not hereafter renounce Thee, for fear of suffering for Thee, but may stand firm in the "day of my visitation."

O Thou Who didst not please Thyself, although for Thy "pleasure all things are and were created," let some portion of Thy Spirit descend on me, that I may "deny myself and follow Thee." Strengthen my soul, that I may be temperate in all things; that I may never use any of Thy creatures but in order to some end Thou commandest me to pursue, and in that measure and manner which most conduces to it. Let me never gratify any desire which has not Thee for its ultimate object. Let me ever abstain from all pleasures which do not prepare me for taking pleasure in Thee; as knowing that all such war against the soul and tend to alienate it from Thee. O save me from ever indulging either "the desire of the flesh, the desire of the eye, or the pride of life." Set a watch, O Lord, over my senses and appetites, my passions and understanding, that I may resolutely deny them every gratification which has no tendency to Thy glory. O train me up in this good way, "that when I am old I may not depart from it"; that I may be at length of a truly mortified heart, "crucified unto the world, and the world crucified unto me."

Hear also my prayers for all mankind and guide their feet into the way of peace; for Thy holy catholic [universal] church—let her live by Thy Spirit, and reign in Thy glory. Remember that branch of it which Thou has planted in these kingdoms, especially the stewards of Thy holy mysteries; give them such zeal, and diligence, and wisdom, that they may save both themselves and those that hear them.

Preserve, O great King of heaven and earth, all Christian Princes, especially our Sovereign and his family. Grant that his Council and all that are in authority under him, may truly and indifferently administer justice. And to all Thy people give Thy heavenly grace, that they may faithfully serve Thee all the days of their life. Bless the Universities with prudence, unity, and holiness. However the way of truth be evil spoken of, may they walk in it even to the end. Whosoever forget or blaspheme their high calling. May they ever remember that they are a "chosen generation, a royal priesthood, a holy nation, peculiar people"; and accordingly "show forth the praise of Him who hath called them out of darkness into His marvelous light."

With a propitious eye, O gracious Lord, behold all my enemies, and all that are in affliction; give them patience under their suffering, and grant that they, and all the members of Thy church may find rest, "where the wicked cease from troubling," and mercy in the great day of trial. In particular, I commend to Thy mercy, my father and mother, my brethren and sisters, my friends and relations [names]. Lord, Thou best knowest all their wants; O suit Thy blessings to their several necessities.

Let these my prayers, O Lord, find access to the throne of grace, through the Son of Thy love, Jesus Christ the righteous; to Whom with Thee, O Father, in the unity of the Spirit, be all love and obedience now and forever!

Wednesday Evening

Particular Questions Relating to Mortification

1. Have I done anything merely because it was pleasing [to me]?
2. Have I not only not done what passion solicited me to, but done just the contrary?
3. Have I received the inconveniences I could not avoid as means of mortification chosen for me by God?
4. Have I contrived pretenses to avoid self-denial? In particular,
5. Have I thought any occasion of denying myself too small to be embraced?
6. Have I submitted my will to the will of every one that opposed it, except where the glory of God was concerned?
7. Have I set apart some time for endeavoring after a lively sense of the sufferings of Christ and my own sins? For deprecating God's judgment, and thinking how to amend?

O Almighty Lord of heaven and earth, I desire with fear and shame to cast myself down before Thee, humbly confessing my manifold sins and unsufferable wickedness I confess, O great God, that I have sinned grievously against Thee by thought, word, and deed, particularly this day. Thy words and Thy laws, O God, are holy and Thy judgments are terrible! But I have broken all Thy righteous laws, and incurred Thy severest judgments; and where shall I appear when Thou are angry?

But, O Lord, my Judge, Thou art also my Redeemer! I have sinned, but Thou, O blessed Jesus, art my Advocate! "Enter not into judgment with me," lest I die; but spare me, gracious Lord, "spare thy servant, whom Thou hast redeemed with Thy most precious blood." O reserve not evil in store for me against the day of vengeance, but let Thy mercy be magnified upon me. Deliver me from the power of sin and preserve me from the punishment of it.

Thou Whose mercy is without measure, Whose goodness is unspeakable, despise not Thy returning servant, who earnestly begs for pardon and reconciliation. Grant me the forgiveness of what is past, and a perfect repentance of all my sins; that for the time to come I may with a pure spirit do Thy will, O God, walking humbly with Thee, conversing charitably with men, possessing my soul in resignation and holiness and my body in sanctification and honor.

"My Lord and my God," I know that unless I am planted together with Thee in the likeness of Thy death, I cannot in the likeness of Thy resurrection. O strengthen me, that by "denying the old man," and utterly destroy the whole body of sin. Give me grace to "mortify all my members which are upon the earth," all my works and affections which are according to corrupt nature. Let me be dead unto sin, unto every transgression of Thy law, which is holy, merciful and perfect. Let me be dead to the world, and all that is in the world, "the desire of the flesh, the desire of the eye, and the pride of life." Let me be dead unto pleasure, so far as it tendeth not to Thee and to those pleasures which are at Thy right hand for evermore. Let me be dead unto my own will, and alive only unto Thine. I am not my own; Thou hast "bought me with a price," with the price of Thine own blood. And Thou didst therefore die for all, "that we should not henceforth live unto ourselves, but unto Him that died for us." Arm Thou me with this mind; circumcise my heart and make me a new creature. Let me no longer live to the desires of men, but to the will of God. Let Thy Holy Spirit enable me to say with Thy blessed Apostle, "I am crucified with Christ, nevertheless I live; yet not I, but Christ in me."

O Thou Great Shepherd of souls, bring home unto Thy fold all that are gone astray. Preserve Thy church from all heresy, and schism, from all that persecute or oppose the truth; and give unto Thy ministers wisdom and holiness, and the powerful aid of Thy blessed Spirit. Advance the just interests, and preserve the persons, of all Christian Princes, especially our

Sovereign: Give him and his Royal Family, and to all his subjects, in their several stations, particularly those that are in authority among them, grace to do Thy will in this world, and eternal glory in the world to come.

Bless, O Lord, all our nurseries of piety and schools of learning, that they may devote all their studies to Thy glory. Have mercy on all that are in affliction; remember the poor and needy, the widow and fatherless, the friendless and oppressed; heal the sick and languishing, give them a sanctified use of Thy rod, and when Thou seest it expedient for them, receive them into the number of Thy departed saints, with them into Thine everlasting kingdom.

O my God, I praise Thee for Thy continued preservation of me, for Thy fatherly protection over me this day; [name] for all the comforts with which Thou surroundest me, spiritual and temporal; particularly for leave now to pray unto Thee. O accept the poor services, pardon the sinfulness of this and all my holy duties, and bless me, my friends, and relations, my benefactors and mine enemies (this night and ever) with the blessings of Thy children.

These my prayers, O most merciful Father, vouchsafe to hear, through the mediation of Jesus Christ our Redeemer; Who with Thee and the Holy Ghost is worshipped and glorified, in all churches of the saints, one God blessed forever!

Thursday Morning

O Eternal God, my Sovereign Lord, I acknowledge all I am, all I have, is Thine. O give me such a sense of Thy infinite goodness, that I may return to Thee all possible love and obedience.

I humbly and heartily thank Thee for all the favors Thou hast bestowed upon me; for creating me after Thine own image, for Thy daily preserving me by Thy good providence, for redeeming me by the death of Thy blessed Son, and for the assistance of Thy Holy Spirit; for causing me to be born in a Christian country, for blessing me with plentiful means of salvation, with religious parents and friends, and frequent returns of Thy ever blessed sacrament. I also thank Thee for all Thy temporal blessings; for the preservation of me this night [name], for my health, strength, food, raiment, and all the comforts and necessities of life. O may I always delight to "praise Thy holy name," and above all Thy benefits love Thee my great Benefactor.

And, O Father of mercies, shut not up Thy bowels of compassion towards me, a vile and miserable sinner; despise not the work of Thine own hands, the purchase of Thy Son's blood. For His sake I most humbly implore forgiveness of all my sins. "Lo, I come now, to do Thy will alone"; and am resolved, by Thy assistance, to have no longer any choice of my own, but with singleness of heart to obey Thy good pleasure; "Father, not my will, but Thine be done," in all my thoughts, words, and actions.

O Thou all-sufficient God of angels and men, Who art above all, and through all, and in all; from Whom, by Whom, and in Whom are all things; —"in Whom we live, move, and have our being;" may my will be as entirely and continually derived from Thine, as my being and happiness are!

I believe, O sovereign Goodness, O mighty Wisdom, that Thou dost sweetly order and govern all things, even the most minute, even the most noxious, to Thy glory, and the good of those that love Thee. I believe, O Father, of the families of heaven and earth, that Thou are disposest all events, as may best magnify Thy goodness to all Thy children, especially those whose eyes wait upon Thee. I most humbly beseech Thee, teach me to wait upon Thee. I most humbly beseech Thee, teach me to adore all Thy ways, though I cannot comprehend them; teach me to be glad that Thou art King, and to give Thee thanks for all things that befall me; seeing Thou hast chosen that for me, and hast thereby "set Thy seal that they are good." And for that which is to come, give me Thy grace to do in all things what pleaseth Thee; and then, with an absolute submission to Thy wisdom, to leave the issues of them in Thy hand.

O Lord Jesu, I give Thee my body, my soul, my substance, my fame, my friends, my liberty, my life; Dispose of me, and my fame, my friends, my liberty, my life; Dispose of me, and all that is mine, as it seemeth best unto Thee. I am not mine, but Thine; Claim me as Thy right, keep me as Thy charge, love me as Thy child! Fight for me when I am assaulted, heal me when I am wounded, and revive me when I am destroyed.

O help me with Thy grace, that whatsoever I shall do for suffer this day may tend to Thy glory. Keep me in love to Thee, and to all men. Do Thou direct my paths, and teach me to set Thee always before me. Let not the things of this life, or my manifold concerns therein, alienate any part of my affections from Thee; nor let me ever pursue or regard them, but for Thee, and in obedience to Thy will.

Extend, O Lord, Thy pity to the whole race of mankind; enlighten the Gentile with Thy truth, and bring into Thy flock Thy ancient people the Jews. Be gracious to the holy catholic [universal] Church; and grant she may always preserve that doctrine and discipline which Thou hast delivered to her. Grant that all of this nation, especially our Governors and the Clergy, may "whatsoever they do, do all to Thy glory." Bless all nurseries of true religion and useful learning and let them not neglect the end of their institution. Be merciful to all that are in distress, [names] that struggle with pain, poverty, or reproach; be Thou a Guide to them that travel by land or by water; give a strong and quiet spirit to those who are condemned to death, liberty to prisoners, and captives, and ease and cheerfulness to every sad heart. O give spiritual strength and comfort to scrupulous consciences, and to them that are afflicted by evil spirits. Pity idiots and lunatics, and give life and salvation to all who Thou hast given no understanding. Give to all that are in error the light of Thy truth; bring all sinners to repentance, [names] and give to all heretics humility and grace to make amends to the church, by the public acknowledgment of an holy faith. Bless all my friends and relations, acquaintance and enemies; [names] unite us all to one another together with all those who are gone before us in Thy faith and fear, may find a merciful acceptance in the last day, through the merits of Thy blessed Son; to Whom with Thee and the Holy Ghost be all glory, world without end!

Thursday Evening

Particular Questions Relating to Resignation and Meekness

1. Have I endeavored to will what God wills, and that only?
2. Have I received everything that has befallen me without my choice, as the choice of infinite wisdom and goodness for me, with thanks?
3. Have I (after doing what He requires of me to do concerning them) left all future things absolutely to God's disposal; that is, have I labored to be wholly indifferent to whichsoever way He shall ordain for me?
4. Have I resumed my claim to my body, soul, friends, fame, or fortune, which I have made over to God; or repented of my gift, when God accepted any of them at my hands?

5. Have I endeavored to be cheerful, mild, and courteous in whatever I said or did?
6. Have I said anything with a stern look, accent, or gesture? Particularly with regard to religion?

My Lord and my God, Thou seest my heart, and my desires are not hid from Thee. I am encouraged by my happy experiences of Thy goodness, (particularly this day past), to present myself before Thee, notwithstanding I know myself unworthy of the least favor from Thee. I am ashamed when I think how long I have lived a stranger, yea, an enemy to Thee, taking upon me to dispose of myself, and to please myself in the main course of my life. But I now unfeignedly desire to return unto Thee, and, renouncing all interest and propriety in myself, to give myself up entirely to Thee; I would be Thine, and only Thine forever. But I know I am nothing, and can do nothing of myself; and if ever I am Thine, I must be wholly indebted to Thee for it. O my God, my Savior, my Sacrifice, turn not away Thy face from a poor soul that seeks Thee; but as Thou hast kindled in me these desires, so confirm, increase, and satisfy them. Reject not that poor gift which I would make of myself unto Thee, but teach me so to make it, that it may be acceptable to Thy sight. Lord, hear me, help me, and show mercy unto me for Jesus Christ's sake.

To Thee, O God, Father, Son and Holy Ghost, my Creator, Redeemer, and Sanctifier, I give up myself entirely: May I no longer serve myself, but Thee, all the days of my life.

I give Thee my understanding: May it be my only care to know Thee, Thy perfections, Thy works, and Thy will. Let all things else be as dung and dross unto me, for the excellency of this knowledge. And let me silence all reasons against whatsoever Thou teachest me, Who cast neither deceive, nor be deceived.

I give Thee my will: May I have no will of my own; whatsoever Thou willest may I will, and that only. May I will Thy glory in all things, as Thou doest, and make that my end in everything; may I ever say with the Psalmist, "Whom have I in heaven but Thee? And there is none upon earth that I desire beside Thee." May I delight to do Thy will, O God, and rejoice to suffer it. Whatever threatens me, let me say, "It is the Lord, let Him do what seemeth [to] Him good"; and whatever befalls me, let me give thanks, since it is Thy will concerning me.

I give Thee my affection: Do Thou dispose of them all; be Thou my love, my fear, my joy; and may nothing have any share in them, but with respect to Thee and for Thy sake. What Thou lovest, may I love; what Thou hatest, may I hate; and that in such measures as Thou art pleased to prescribe me.

I give Thee my body; May I glorify Thee with it, and preserve it holy, fit for thee, O God, to dwell in. May I neither indulge it, nor use too much rigor towards it but keep it, as far as in me lies, healthy, vigorous, and active, and fit to do Thee all manner of services which Thou shalt call for.

I give Thee all my worldly goods; May I prize them and use them only for Thee; May I faithfully restore to Thee, in the poor, all Thou hast entrusted me with, above the necessities of life; and be content to part with them too, whenever Thou, my Lord, shalt require them at my hands.

I give Thee my credit and reputation: May I never value it, but only in respect of Thee; nor endeavor to maintain it, but as it may do Thee service and advance Thy honor in the world.

I give Thee myself and my all; Let me look upon myself to be nothing, and to have nothing, out of Thee. Be Thou the sole disposer and governor of myself and all; be Thou my portion and my all.

O my God and my all, when hereafter I shall be tempted to break this solemn engagement, when I shall be pressed to conform to the world, and to the company and customs that surround me; may my answer be, "I am not my own; I am not for myself, nor for the world, but for my God. I will give unto God the things which are God's. God be merciful to me a sinner."

Have mercy, O Father of the spirits of all flesh, on all mankind. Convert all Jews, Turks, and Heathens, to Thy truth. Bless the catholic [universal Christian] Church; heal its breaches, and establish it in truth and peace. Preserve and defend all Christians, Princes, especially our Sovereign and his family. Be merciful to the nation; bless the Clergy with soundness of doctrine and purity of life, the Council with wisdom, the Magistrates with integrity and zeal, and the people with loyalty. Bless the Universities with learning and holiness, that they may afford a constant supply of men fit and able to do Thee service.

Shower down Thy graces on all my relations, on all my friends, and all that belong to this family. Comfort and relieve those that labor under an affliction of body or mind, especially those who suffer for the testimony of a good conscience. Visit them, O gracious Lord, in all their distresses. Thou knowest, Thou seest, them under all. O stay their souls upon Thee; give them to rejoice that they are counted worthy to suffer for Thy name's sake, and constantly to look unto the author and finisher of their faith. Supply abundantly to all their souls who are in prison, the want of Thy holy ordinances, and in Thy good time, deliver them, and be merciful unto them, as Thou usest to be unto them that love Thy name. Those that love or do good to me, reward sevenfold into their bosom [names] those that hate me [names] convert and forgive; and grant us all, together with Thy whole Church, an entrance into Thine everlasting kingdom, through Jesus Christ; to whom with Thee and the blessed Spirit, three Persons and one God, be ascribed all majesty, dominion, and power, now and for evermore. Amen.

Friday Morning

Almighty and everlasting God, I bless Thee from my heart, that of Thy infinite goodness Thou hast preserved me this night past, and hast, with the impregnable defense of Thy providence, protested me from the power and malice of the devil. Withdraw not, I humbly entreat Thee, Thy protection from me. But mercifully this day watch over me with the eyes of Thy mercy. Direct my soul and body according to the rule of Thy will, and fill my heart with Thy Holy Spirit, that I may pass this day, and all the rest of my days, to Thy glory.

O Savior of the world, God of gods, light of light; Thou art the brightness of Thy Father's glory, the express image of His person; Thou that hast destroyed the power of the devil, that hast overcome death, "that sittest at the right hand of the Father," Thou wilt speedily come down in Thy Father's glory to judge all men according to their works: Be Thou my light and my peace; destroy the power of the devil in me, and make me a new creature. O Thou Who didst cast seven devils out of Mary Magdalene, cast out of my heart all corrupt affections. O Thou Who didst raise Lazarus from the dead, raise me from the death of sin. Thou Who didst cleanse the lepers, heal the sick, and give sight to the blind, heal the disease of my soul; open my eyes, and fix them singly on the prize of my high calling, and cleanse my heart from every desire but that of advancing Thy glory.

O Jesus, poor and abject, unknown and despised, have mercy upon me, and let me not be ashamed to follow Thee. O Jesus, hated, calumniated, and persecuted, have mercy upon me, and let me not be ashamed to come after Thee. O Jesus, betrayed and sold at a vile price, have mercy upon me, and make me content to be as my Master. O Jesus, blasphemed, accursed and wrongfully condemned, have mercy upon me, and teach me to endure the contradictions of sinners. O Jesus, clothed with a habit of reproach and shame, have mercy upon me, and let me not seek my own glory. O Jesus, insulted, mocked, and spit upon, have mercy upon me, and let me run with patience the race that is set before me. O Jesus, dragged to the pillar, scourged, and bathed in blood, have mercy on me, and let me not faint in the fiery trial. O Jesus, crowned with thorns, and hailed in derision; O Jesus, burdened with our sins, and the curses of the people; O Jesus, affronted, outraged, buffeted, overwhelmed with injuries, griefs, and humiliations; O Jesus, hanging on the accursed tree, bowing the head, giving up the ghost, have mercy upon me, and conform my whole soul to Thy holy, humble, suffering Spirit. O Thou who for the love of me hast undergone such an infinity of sufferings, and humiliations, let me be wholly "emptied of myself," that I may rejoice to take up my cross daily and follow Thee. Enable me, too, to endure the pain and despise the shame; and, if be Thy will, to resist even unto blood!

Holy, holy, holy, Lord God Almighty, I, miserable sinner, humbly acknowledge that I am altogether unworthy to pray for myself. But since Thou hast commanded me to make prayers and intercessions for all men, in obedience to Thy command, and confidence of Thy unlimited goodness, I commend to Thy mercy the wants and necessities of all mankind. Lord, let it be Thy good pleasure to restore to Thy Church catholic [universal], primitive peace and purity; to show mercy to these sinful nations, and give us grace at length to break off our sins by repentance; defend our Church from all the assaults of schism, heresy, and sacrilege; and bless all Bishops, Priests, and Deacons with apostolical graces. O let it be Thy good pleasure to defend the King from all his enemies, spiritual and temporal; to bless all his royal relations; to grant to the Council wisdom, to the Magistrates zeal and prudence, to the Gentry and Commons piety and loyalty!

Lord, let it be Thy good pleasure to give Thy grace to the Universities; to bless those whom I have wronged, [names] and to forgive those who have wronged me; [names] to comfort the disconsolate, to give health and patience to all that are sin and afflicted [names].

Vouchsafe to bless my father and mother with the fear of Thy name, that they may be holy in all manner of conversation. Let them remember how short their time is and be careful to improve every moment of it. O Thou Who hast kept them from their youth up until now, forsake them not now they are grey headed, but perfect them in every good word and work, and be Thou their Guide unto death. Bless my brethren and sisters, whom Thou hast graciously taught the gospel of Thy Christ; give them further degrees of illumination, that they may serve Thee with a perfect heart and willing mind. Bless my friends and benefactors, and all who have commended themselves to my prayers [names]. Lord, Thou best knowest all our conditions, all our desires, all our wants. O do Thou suit Thy grace and blessings to all our several necessities.

Hear, O merciful Father, my supplications, for the sake of Thy Son Jesus; and bring us, with all those who have pleased Thee from the beginning of the world, into the glories of Thy Son's kingdom: To whom with Thee and the Holy Ghost, be all praise forever and ever! "Our Father," and etc.

Friday Evening

Particular Questions Relating to Mortification

1. Have I done anything merely because it was pleasing [to me]?
2. Have I not only not done what passion solicited me to, but done just the contrary?
3. Have I received the inconveniences I could not avoid as means of mortification chosen for me by God?
4. Have I contrived pretenses to avoid self-denial? In particular,
5. Have I thought any occasion of denying myself too small to be embraced?
6. Have I submitted my will to the will of every one that opposed it, except where the glory of God was concerned?
7. Have I set apart some time for endeavoring after a lively sense of the sufferings of Christ and my own sins? For deprecating God's judgment, and thinking how to amend?

O God the Father, Who canst not be thought to have made me only to destroy me, have mercy upon me.

O God the Son, Who knowing Thy Father's will, didst come into the world to save me, have mercy upon me.

O God the Holy Ghost, Who to the same end hast so often since breathed holy thoughts into me, have mercy upon me.

O holy, blessed, and glorious Trinity, Whom in three Persons I adore as one God, have mercy upon me.

Lord, carest Thou not that I perish? Thou that wouldest have all men to be saved? Thou that wouldest have no to perish? And wilt Thou now show Thine anger against a worm, a leaf? Against a vapor that vanisheth before Thee? O remember how short my time is and deliver not my souls into the power of hell. For, alas, what profit is there in my blood? Or, who shall give Thee thanks in that pit? No; let me live in Thy sight: Let me live, O my God, and my soul shall praise Thee. Forget me as I have been disobedient, provoking Thee to anger; and regard me as I am distressed, crying out to Thee for help. Look not upon me as I am a sinner; but consider me as I am Thy creature. A sinner I am, I confess, a sinner of no ordinary stain: But let not this hinder Thee, O my God; for upon such sinners Thou gettest the greatest glory.

O remember for whose sake it was that Thou camest from the bosom of Thy Father, and wast content to be born of Thine own handmaid. Remember for whom it was that Thy tender body was torn and scourged and crucified. Was it not for the sins of the whole world? And shall I be so injurious to Thy glory, as to think Thou hast excepted me? Or can I think, Thou didst only for sinners of a lower kind, and leftist such as me without remedy? What had become then of him who filled Jerusalem with blood? What had become then of her, who lived in a trade of sin? Nay, what had become of Thine own disciple, who with oaths and curses thrice denied Thee?

O, how easy is it for Thee to forgive! For it is Thy nature. How proper is it for Thee to save! For it is Thy name. How suitable is it to Thy coming into the world! For it is Thy business. And when I consider that I am the chief of sinners, may I not urge Thee farther, and say, Shall the chief of Thy business be left undone? Far be that from Thee! Have mercy upon me!

I ask not of Thee the things of this world, give them to whom Thou pleases, so Thou givest me mercy. O say unto my soul, "Be of good cheer; thy sins are forgiven thee." O that I might never sin against Thee more! And wheresoever my conscience accuses me most, be Thou most merciful unto me.

Save me, O God, as a brand snatched out of the fire.

Receive me, O my Savior, as a sheep that is gone astray, but would now return to the great Shepherd and Bishop of my soul.

Father, accept my imperfect repentance, compassionate my infirmities, forgive my wickedness, purify my uncleanness, strengthen my weakness, fix my unstableness, and let Thy good Spirit watch over me forever, and Thy love ever rule in my heart, through the merits and sufferings and love of Thy Son, in Whom Thou art always well pleased.

Give Thy grace, O holy Jesus, to all the world; and let all Who are redeemed by Thy blood, acknowledge Thee to be the Lord. Let all Christians, especially those of this nation, keep themselves unspotted from the world. Let all Governors, and especially our Sovereign, rule with wisdom and justice; and let the Clergy be exemplary in their lives, and discreet and diligent in their labors. Let our Universities enjoy freedom from violence and faction and excel in true religion and sound learning. Be a help at hand to all that are afflicted and assist them to trust in Thee. Raise up friends for the widow and the fatherless, the friendless and oppressed. Give patience to all that are sick, comfort to all troubled consciences, strength to all that are tempted. Be gracious to my relations [names] to all that are endeared to me by their kindness or acquaintance, to all who remember me in their prayers, or desire to be remembered in mine [names]. Sanctify, O merciful Lord, the friendship which Thou hast granted me with these Thy servants [names]. O let our prayers be heard for each other, while our hearts are united in Thy fear and love, and graciously unite them therein more and more. Strengthen the hearts of us Thy servants against all our corruptions and temptations; enable us to consecrate ourselves faithfully and entirely to Thy service. Grant that we may "provoke each other to love" and serve Thee and grow up together before Thee in Thy fear and love, to Thy heavenly Kingdom. And by Thy infinite mercies, vouchsafe to bring us, with those that are dead in Thee, to rejoice together before Thee, through the merits of our dear Lord Jesus Christ; to Whom, with Thee and the Holy Ghost, the blessed and only Potentate, the King of kings, and Lord of lords, be honor and power everlasting.

Saturday Morning

O God, Thou great Creator and Sovereign Lord of heaven and earth, Thou Father of angels and men, Thou Giver of life and Protector of all Thy creatures, mercifully accept this my morning sacrifice of praise and thanksgiving, which I desire to offer, with all humility, to Thy divine Majesty. "Thou are praised, O Lord, by all Thy works," and magnified by everything which Thou has created. The sun rejoiceth to run his course, that he may set forth Thy praise Who madest him. Nor to the moon and stars refrain to manifest Thy glory, even amidst the silent night. The earth breathes forth each day perfumes, as incense to Thee, her sacred King, Who has crowned her with herbs and trees, and beautified her with hills and dales. The deep uttereth His voice, and lifteth up His hands on high to Thee, the great Creator, the universal King, the everlasting God. The floods clap their hands, and the hills are joyful together before Thee: the fruitful vales rejoice and sing Thy praise. Thou feedest the innumerable multitude of animals which Thou hast created; "These all wait upon Thee, and Thou madest light for them their meat in due season." Thou madest light for our comfort, and brought-est forth darkness out of Thy treasures to overshadow the earth, that the living creatures of it might take their rest. "The fire and hail, snow and vapor, wind and storm, fulfill Thy word," and manifest Thy glory. Inanimate things declare Thee, O Lord of life; and irrational animals demonstrate their Wise Creator. Amidst this universal jubilee of nature, suffer not, I beseech Thee, the sons of men to be silent; but let the noblest work of Thy creation pay Thee the noblest sacrifice of praise. O pour Thy grace into my heart, that I may worthily magnify Thy great and glorious name. Thou hast made me and sent me into the world to do Thy work. O assist me to fulfill the end of my creation, and to show forth Thy praises with all diligence, by giving myself up to Thy service. Prosper the work of my hands upon me, O Lord; O prosper Thou whatever I shall undertake this day, that it may tend to Thy glory, the good of my neighbor, and the salvation of my own soul.

Preserve me from all those snares and temptations which continually solicit me to offend Thee. Guide me by Thy Holy Spirit in all those places whither Thy providence shall lead me this day; and suffer not my commu-nications with the world to dissipate my thoughts, to make me inadvertent to Thy presence, or lukewarm in Thy service; but let me always walk as in Thy sight, and as one who knows this life to be the seed-time of an eternal harvest. Keep me, I beseech Thee, undefiled, unblameable, and unreprove-able unto the end; and grant that I may so diligently perform Thy will, in that station wherein Thou hast been pleased to place me, that I may make my calling and election sure, through Jesus Christ, our blessed Lord and Servant.

Hear also, O Lord, my prayers for the whole race of mankind, and guide their feet into the way of peace. Reform the corruptions of Thy catholic [universal] Church, heal her divisions, and restore to her her ancient discipline; give to the Clergy thereof, whether they be Bishops, Priests, or Deacons, grace, as good shepherds, to feed the flocks committed to their charge. Bless King George and all the Royal Family, and all that are put in authority under him. Let them exceed others as much in goodness as greatness and be signal instruments of Thy glory. Grant that in the Universities, and in all other places set apart for Thy service, whatsoever is praiseworthy may forever flourish. Keep, O Lord, all the Nobility, Gentry, and Commons of this land, in constant communion with Thy holy catholic [universal] Church, in humble obedience to the King, and in Christian charity one towards another.

In a particular manner, I beseech Thee to be gracious to my father and mother, my brethren and sisters, and all my friends and relations. Pardon all their sins and heal all their infirmities. Give them that share of the blessings of this life, which Thou knowest to be the most expedient for them; and Thy graces so to use them here, that they may enjoy Thee eternally.

With a propitious eye, O gracious Comforter, behold all that are in affliction; let the sighings of the prisoners, the groans of the sick, the prayers of the oppressed, the desire of the poor and needy, come before thee [names]. Give unto my enemies [names] grace and pardon, charity to me and love to Thee; remove the cloud from their eyes, the stony from their hearts, that they may know and feel what it is to love their neighbor as themselves. And may it please Thee to enable me to love all mine enemies, to bless them that now curse me, to do good to them that hate me, and to pray for those who despitefully use me and persecute me. Be please, O Lord, of Thy goodness, shortly to accomplish the number of Thine elect, and to hasten Thy kingdom; that we, with all Thy whole Church, may have our perfect consummation of bliss, through Jesus Christ our Lord; by whom, and with whom, in the unity of the Holy Ghost, all honor and glory be unto Thee, O Father Almighty, now and forever.

Saturday Evening

Particular Questions Relating to Thankfulness

1. Have I allotted some time for thanking God for the blessings of the past week?

2. Have I, in order to be the more sensible of them, seriously and deliberately considered the several circumstances that attended them?

3. Have I considered each of them as an obligation to greater love, and consequently, to stricter holiness?

O most great and glorious God, Who art mighty to Thy power, and wonderful in Thy doings towards the sons of men, accept, I beseech Thee, my unfeigned thanks and praise for my creation, preservation, and all the other blessings which, in the riches of Thy mercy, Thou hast from time to time poured down upon me. "Thou, Lord, in the beginning hast laid the foundation of the earth, and the heavens are the works of Thine hand." Thou created the sun and moon, the day and the night, and makest the outgoings of the morning and the evening to praise Thee. Thou "formedst man of the dust of the ground and breathed into him the breath of life." In Thine own image madest Thou him, capable of knowing and loving Thee eternally. His nature was perfect, Thy will was his law and Thy blessed self his portion. Neither after he had left his first estate didst Thou utterly withdraw Thy mercy from him; but, in every succeeding generation, didst save, deliver, assist, and protect him. Thou hast instructed us by Thy laws and enlightened us by Thy statutes; Thou hast redeemed us by the blood of Thy Son, and sanctifiest us by the grace of Thy Holy Spirit. For these and all Thy other mercies, how can I sufficiently love Thee, or worthily magnify Thy great and glorious name? All the powers of my soul are too vouchsafing me the honor of now appearing before Thee and conversing with Thee. But thou hast declared Thou wilt accept the sacrifice of thanksgiving in return for all Thy goodness. For ever therefore will I bless Thee, will I adore Thy power, and magnify Thy goodness; "My tongue shall sing of Thy righteousness, and be telling of Thy salvation from day to day." I will give thanks unto Thee forever and ever; I will praise my god while I have my being. O that I had the heart of the seraphim, that I might burn with love like theirs. But though I am upon earth, yet will I praise, as I can, the King of Heaven; though I am a feeble, mortal creature, yet will I join my song with those that excel in strength, with the immortal host of angels, and archangels, thrones, dominions, and powers, while they laud and magnify Thy glorious name, and sing with incessant shouts of praise—

"Holy, holy, holy is the Lord of Hosts! Heaven and earth are full of His glory! Glory be to Thee, O Lord most high. Amen. Hallelujah."

Accept, O merciful Father, my most humble thanks for Thy preservation of me this day [name]. O Continue Thy loving kindness towards me and take me into Thy protection this night. Let Thy holy angels watch over me to defend me from the attempts of evil men and evil spirits. Let me rest in peace, and not sleep in sin; and grant that I may rise more fit for Thy service.

O Thou Whose kingdom ruleth over all, rule in the hearts of all the men whom Thou hast made; reform the corruptions, and heal the breaches, of the holy Church, and establish her in truth and peace. Be gracious unto all Priests and Deacons and give them rightly to divide the word of truth. Forgive the sins of this nation, and turn our hearts, that iniquity may not be our ruin. Bless King George, and all the Royal Family, with all those blessings which Thou seest to be most expedient for them; and give to his Council, and to the Nobility and Magistracy, grace truly to serve Thee in their several stations. Bless our Universities, that they may be the great bulwarks of Thy faith and love, against all assaults of vice and infidelity. May the Gentry and Commons of this realm live in constant communion with thy Church, in obedience to the King, and in love one towards another.

Be gracious to all who are near and dear to me. Thou knowest their names, and art acquainted with their wants. Of Thy goodness be pleased to proportion Thy blessings to their necessities. Pardon my enemies, and give them repentance and charity, and me grace to overcome evil with good. Have compassion on all who are distressed in mind, body, or estate, and give them steady patience, and timely deliverance.

Now, to God the Father, Who first love us, and made us accepted in the Beloved; to God the Son, Who loved us, and washed us from our sins in His own blood; to God the Holy Ghost, who sheddeth the love of God abroad in our hearts, be all love and all glory in time and to all eternity. Amen.

Appendix B

Selected Prayers by Susanna Wesley

True Religion[1]

Help me, Lord to remember that religion is not to be confined to the church or closet, nor exercised only in prayer and meditation, but that everywhere I am in Thy presence. So that my every word and action have a moral content.

As defects and infirmities betray themselves in the daily accidents and common conversations of my life, grant me Thy grace, O Lord, that I may watch over, regulate and govern them. Enable me to know myself and those whom I have to do, that I may conform to the precepts of the gospel and train myself to those rules of wisdom, and virtue of which I am capable.

Help me to discern the proper season and the just occasion of every virtue, and then to apply myself to attain it, by exercising it in those beneficent activities which, for want [lack] of due reflection, may not seem of any real importance.

May all the things of my life instruct me and afford me an opportunity of exercising some virtue and daily learning and growing toward Thy likeness, and let the world go which way it will. Amen.

---

1   W. L. Doughty, ed., *The Prayers of Susanna Wesley* (Grand Rapids, MI: Zondervan, 1984), 1–2. The title was added.

Fortify My Mind[2]

Help me, O god, to fortify my mind with patience, submission and renewed repentance, that I may be assured of divine succors when I most need them.

Enable me to live so as to deserve a friend, and if I never have one on earth, be Thou my friend, for in having Thee I shall have all that is dear and valuable in friendship. May I learn by practice to love Thee above all things, so that I may be out of the power of the world and my earthly circumstances give me no uneasiness.

I would have my wealth to be Thy favor, with all the blessed consequences attending it; the virtues of Thy Holy Spirit, purifying my mind, exalting my nature to the dignity of a divine resemblance, teaching me to undervalue whatever a mistaken world calls good, as unnecessary or a hindrance to that spiritual and eternal good that I would prize above all others.

Though a good name is as precious as precious ointment, yet I remember that I have offered up mine to Thee, my God, and have resolved never to make my reputation or the esteem of man the end of any of my actions, where Thy glory is not concerned.

So I trust Thee with the conduct of my soul, committing myself to Thee in ways of well-doing, praying that Thou will not suffer me to do anything that would reasonably reflect upon my Christian profession, but enable me to scorn the reputation of any quality or virtue that terminated in myself.

Help me, O Lord, to do well. Amen.

Our First Duty[3]

Almighty God, the Great Father of Spirits, You made us Yourself; and You know perfectly the works of Your own omnipotence. You know the powers of our minds, their various motions and springs of action.

---

2   Doughty, ed., 3–4.

3   Michael McMullen, ed., *Prayers and Meditations of Susanna Wesley* (Peterborough, UK: The Methodist Publishing House, 2000), 27.

You have required that the first instance of our duty toward You must be that we love the Lord our God with all the heart, with all the mind, with all the soul, and with all the strength we have. Amen.

Freedom of Mind[4]

Be pleased, O God, to grant me that great freedom of mind that will enable me to follow and attend on Jesus with a pure heart; to be ever prepared and disposed to observe His example and obey His precepts.

And do Thou further help me to achieve that consummate prudence, great purity, great separation from the world, much liberty and a firm and steadfast faith in the Lord Jesus that will enable me to manage the common affairs of life in such a way as not to misemploy or neglect the improvement of my talents; to be industrious without covetousness; diligent without anxiety; as exact in each detail of action as if success were dependent on it, and yet so resigned as to leave all events to Thee and still attributing to Thee the praise of every good work. Amen.

My Peace and Happiness[5]

I have found, O God, that my peace and happiness depend much on my own opinion of myself and not on that of others. It is the inward sentiments I have of myself that raise or deject me; and my mind can no more be pleased with any sensation but its own than the body can be gratified by the relishes of another palate.

Save me from leading an imaginary life in the ideas of others, and so to be eager and forward in showing myself to the world. Forbid that I should retain, improve and adorn this fictitious being, while stupidly neglecting the true.

Help me not to contend with men's interests, prejudices, and passions, that rarely admit of a calm dispute, when it can innocently be avoided. May I be so far a lover of myself as to prefer the peace and tranquility of my own mind before that of others, and if, after doing all that I can to make others

---

4   Doughty, ed., *The Prayers of Susanna Wesley*, 5–6.

5   Doughty, ed., 7–8.

happy, they yet remain obstinately bent to follow those ways that lead to misery, I leave them to Thy mercy. Amen.

Sincere Devotion[6]

O God, I find it most difficult to preserve a devout and serious temper of mind in the midst of much worldly business.

Were I permitted to choose a state of life, or positively to ask of you anything in this world, I would humbly choose and beg that I might be placed in such a station wherein I might have daily bread with moderate care and that I might have more leisure to retire from the world without injuring those dependent upon me.

Yet I do not know whether such a state of life would really be the best for me; nor am I assured that if I had more leisure I should be more zealously devoted to You and serve You better than now.

Therefore, O Lord, show me that it is undoubtedly best to keep my mind in habitual submission and resignation to You, You who are infinitely, incomprehensively wise and good; Who cannot possibly err, but Who does certainly know what is best for Your children and how and where to fix the bounds of their habitation; Who has given us Your Word, that all things shall work together for good to those that love You; may that Word support and calm my mind in all adverse or uneasy circumstances of life. Amen.

Seeing God in Jesus[7]

Almighty God, inasmuch as I cannot form right apprehensions of Thee by the dim light of nature, I thank Thee because Thou, in Thy mercy and knowing that the happiness of man cannot be secured without that knowledge, hast condescended to reveal that which reason is too weak to discover.

Thou hast directed me and all men to search and find Thee as Thou art in Jesus Christ, in Whom dwelleth the fullness of Thy godhead bodily. For me to know our Lord only as a man is to learn that I have done, and daily do, many things contrary to Thy divine nature and the dictates of my own reason, which must necessarily lead me to despair.

---

6   McMullen, ed., *Prayers and Meditations*, 57.
7   Doughty, ed., *Prayers of Susanna Wesley*, 11–12.

But to behold Thee in Jesus Christ, reconciling the world unto Thyself; by faith to see Thee, the infinite, all-glorious Being, assuming the character of a Savior, a repairer of the lapses and healer of the diseases and miseries of mankind, penetrates and melts my soul. It is something my heart feels and labors under, but my tongue cannot express.

I adore Thee, O God! I adore! Amen.

Taking Up Our Cross[8]

He that sits on the throne shall feed us and shall lead us unto living fountains of water. Far be from us to think that the grace of god can be purchased with anything less precious than the blood of Jesus.

But if it could, who that has the lowest degree of faith would not part with all things in this world to obtain that love for our dear Redeemer which we so long for and sigh after?

Here we cannot watch one hour with Jesus without weariness; failure of spirits, dejection of mind, worldly regards which damp our devotions; and pollute the purity of our sacrifices.

And what Christian does not often feel and bewail the weighty corrupt nature and the many infirmities which molest us in our way to glory? And how difficult is it to practice as we ought that great duty of self-denial, to take up our cross; and follow the Captain of our salvation, without ever repining or murmuring.

If shame or confusion could not enter those blessed mansions, how would our souls be ashamed and confounded at the review of our imperfect services when we see them crowned with such an unprofitable reward? How shall we blush! Amen.

The Most Powerful Teacher[9]

Lord, my mind is naturally so corrupted and all the powers thereof so weakened that I cannot possibly aspire vigorously towards You, or have any clear perception of spiritual things without Your assistance.

---

8   McMullen, ed., *Prayers and Meditations*, 65.

9   McMullen, ed., *Prayers and Meditations*, 23.

Therefore, nothing less than the same Almighty power that raised Jesus Christ from the dead can raise my soul from the death of sin to a life of holiness. That is why to know You experimentally is altogether supernatural and something I could never attain to but by the merits and intercession of Jesus Christ.

By virtue of what You have done and suffered and are now doing in heaven for me, You give us your Holy Spirit, Who is the best Instructor and most powerful Teacher I can possibly have, and without Whose agency all other means of grace would be ineffectual.

How certainly does He assist and strengthen my soul; if it is sincere and hearty in its endeavors to avoid any evil or to perform any good! May He enable me to have a good desire and a fervent aspiration toward You, my God, longings that shall not pass unregarded. Amen.

God Who Governs the World[10]

I thank Thee, O God, for the relief and satisfaction of mind that come with the firm assurance that Thou does govern the world: for the patience and resignation to Thy providence that are afforded as I reflect that even the tumultuous and irregular actions of sinful men are, nevertheless, under Thy direction, Who art wise, good, and omnipotent. And hast promised to make all things work together for good to them that love Thee.

Since I must expect to meet with many difficulties, much oppositions, many disappointments, and daily trials of faith, and patience in my passage through this world, may it be my highest wisdom to disengage my affections as much as I lawfully may from all transitory, temporal enjoyments, and to fix them on those more rational and spiritual pleasures that we are to enjoy when we enter on our state of immortality; to endeavor to secure eternal happiness by using my utmost endeavors to gain a treasure that lies beyond the reach of all the storms and tempests of this world; a kingdom that cannot be shaken by faction, cannot be disturbed by ill men; where there are no parties or separate interests to engage or divide men's affections, but all shall perfectly agree to make up a divine harmony of praise and adoration. Amen.

---

10 Doughty, ed., *Prayers of Susanna Wesley*, 15–16.

The Glory of God[11]

There are no words in ours, nor in all the languages on earth whereby to express infinity—but when we consider God's nature—His Being—this includes infinity.

Whatever glory we ascribe to Him such as power, wisdom, justice, goodness, truth and holiness, are not in Him distinct powers or acquired virtues superadded to His essence, they are His very essence itself!

Therefore, though we often call Him a wise, a powerful, a holy, and a just God—He is Wisdom! Power! Justice! Goodness! And Truth! For God is One!

The infinity of God, therefore, tells us that His Being—His essential perfection—is immense! It is without bounds or limits! His power is inexhaustible! His knowledge, wisdom, and goodness are absolutely perfect. Amen.

The Love That Overwhelms Us[12]

Lord, who can think, much less speak, of the vast subject of the Godhead? Your greatness, Your dignity astonishes us! The purity of Your nature and your redeeming love, confounds and overpowers us!

At the perception of Your glory, our feeble powers are suspended, and nature faints before the God of nature. I dare not say I love You, only that I have chosen You for my own happiness, my all, my only good; in a word—for my God.

That You are everywhere present, and we always present to You is certain, but that we should always be able to realize Your presence is quite another thing.

You are so infinitely blessed, so absolutely lovely, that every perception of You, every approach to Your supreme glory and blessedness, impart such a vital joy and gladness to my mind, as banishes all pain and sense of misery, and were eternity added to this happiness, it would be heaven. Amen.

---

11   McMullen, ed., *Prayers and Meditations*, 74.
12   McMullen, ed., 79.

Calamities and Disappointments[13]

Help me, O Lord, to make a true use of all disappointments in this life, in such a way that they may unite my heart more closely with Thee. Cause them to separate my affections from worldly things and inspire my soul with more vigor in the pursuit of true happiness. Until this temper of mind be attained I can never enjoy any settled peace, much less a calm serenity.

Thou only, O God, canst satisfy my immortal soul and bestow those spiritual pleasures that alone are proper to its nature. Grant me grace to stay and center my soul in Thee: to confine its desires, hopes, and expectations of happiness to Thee alone; calmly to attend to the dispensations of Thy providence and to have a firm, habitual resignation to Thy will.

Enable me to love Thee, my God, with all my heart, with all my mind, with all my strength; so love Thee as to desire Thee; so to desire Thee as to be uneasy without Thee, without Thy favor, without some such resemblance to Thee as my nature in this imperfect state can bear. Amen.

The Still, Small Voice[14]

Almighty God, what an exceeding condescension is it for Thy Holy Spirit at any time to grant assistance to a creature so sinful and worthless as I am! Give me grace to be careful lest at any time I should grieve Thee and provoke Thee to depart from me.

May I not despise or neglect the grace by which alone I stand! By that grace may my mind be purified from all that would offend Thee; be kept calm and composed and, as much as possible, separate from the world.

I have found that the still, small voice is not heard amidst the thunder and noise of tumultuous passions. Keep, then, my mind in a temper for recollection. Be pleased, often in the day, to call it in from outward objects, lest it wander into forbidden paths.

Help me to do my duty and to make use of all the means for obtaining Divine grace that Thou doest afford me. I throw myself upon Thy divine

---

13 Doughty, ed., *Prayers of Susanna Wesley,* 19–20.
14 Doughty, ed., 23–24.

goodness for success and firmly reply on the merits of Christ Jesus to supply my deficiencies. Amen.

Compose and Collect My Thoughts[15]

Enable me, O God, to collect and compose my thoughts before an immediate approach to Thee in prayer. May I be careful to have my mind in order when I take upon myself the honor to speak to the sovereign Lord of the universe, remembering that upon the temper of my soul depends, in very great measure, my success.

Thou art infinitely too great to be trifled with; to wise to be imposed on by a mock devotion and dost abhor a sacrifice without a heart.

Help me to entertain an habitual sense of Thy perfections, as an admirable help against cold and formal performances. Save me from engaging in rash and precipitate prayers and from abrupt breaking away to follow business or pleasure, as though I had never prayed. Amen.

Regulate My Passions[16]

Almighty God, inasmuch as we receive knowledge of things about us by our senses, and we cannot wholly prevent the strong temptations that sensual objects are wont to make on the mind, help me to maintain the superiority of my mind over matter, let it be corrupted by too close adherence to sensible things.

Give me power to preserve the government of reason, and not suffer passions to gain the ascendency over me. Very heartily and earnestly do I pray unto Thee, O God, for strength to govern and regulate my passions.

It is not in man that walketh to direct his steps, therefore I humble implore Thee to steer my soul by Thy Holy Spirit through all the intricate scenes of human life. I depend not on my wisdom, believing that Thou wilt guide me by Thy counsel, and at last conduct me to Thy glory, through Jesus Christ our Lord. Amen.

---

15 Doughty, ed., 26.
16 Doughty, ed., 26.

Being Strong in the Lord[17]

Lord, help us all to resolve not to be much concerned at what is met with in this world—however contrary to our present inclinations.

Help us to see that whatever occurs, events are ordered by Your unerring wisdom—as wisdom that disposes of all things; that fixes the bounds; and determines the place of our habitation.

Help us to endure all things with patience as we see the end of all troubles to be at hand, for life passes most quickly.

Remind us that in a few years—perhaps days—we shall pass into another state very different from this, wherein we shall always enjoy that tranquility that is in vain sought for in any temporal employment, nor shall we sin or sorrow more. Help us to encourage each other, then, as we think on eternity. Amen.

Perplexing Affairs of Life[18]

Almighty God, I thank Thee because day after day has verified the truth of our Savior's words: "Sufficient to the day is the evil thereof [Mt. 6:34]." Through the weakness and corruption of human nature and the unavoidable business of my station in life; in many unforeseen accidents and unexpected company; in cross occurrences, with abundance of other things incident to human life, I find occasion given to me daily to exercise virtues of one kind or another.

One day calls me to use justice and patience, and another prudence, temperance, and charity in forgiving injuries. I draw near unto Thee, the Supreme foundation of virtue, for grace in the perplexed affairs of life, and thank Thee for every occasion on which I have found Thy strength to be made perfect in weakness; and I thank Thee that Thou art truth itself and that all Thy promises are yea and amen, through Jesus Christ, Thy Mediator. Amen.

---

17 McMullen, ed., *Prayers and Meditations*, 59; title slightly altered.
18 Doughty, ed., *Prayers of Susanna Wesley*, 27.

Feeling Melancholy and Morose[19]

I thank Thee, O God, because I know that religion does not mean melancholy and moroseness, tending only to destroy the comforts of our environment. But I have learned that all things in the world, where religion is lacking, cannot possibly make people happy or easy to themselves or others.

Whatever I enjoy of the good things of this life is attained with so much vanity and vexation of spirit that my happiness, even in this world, depends entirely on Thy favor.

When I am peevish and morose, it is not because of religion, but my lack of it. Help me not to be discouraged by my own failures, not to spend too much time in thinking on them, remembering that perfection is my Savior's endowment and sincerity is mine. Help me with firm faith to reply on His merits, joined with my sincere endeavor to obey Thy whole will. Amen.

Knowing God[20]

You have taught me, Lord, that to pursue after knowledge only for its own sake, is a vain and unprofitable curiosity. To labor for it only that I may be applauded by others, is still worse, and displays a vainglorious, weak and childish temper.

Such knowledge puffs up and is directly opposite to divine charity—the love of God—which alone edifies or establishes the soul in all Christian virtues.

We must know that we may love, we must love that we may cheerfully obey, and we must obey, that we may please God.

Knowledge that goes no farther than speculation, is like an excellent instrument in the hand of an unskilled person who know not how to make use of it.

The wisdom I earnestly pray for is that wisdom that goes on to practice the general rules it has understood. Amen.

---

19 Doughty, ed., 28, with the vocabulary modernized slightly.

20 McMullen, ed., *Prayers and Meditations*, 26.

Praising the Savior[21]

I thank Thee, O God, for the abundant reason that I have to adore, to praise, to magnify Thy goodness and love in sending Thy Son into the world to die for sinners. What reason have I to praise and adore and love that Savior who suffered so much to redeem me!

What sentiments of gratitude should I conceive for such boundless charity to souls! Help me gladly and cheerfully to take up my cross for Him who suffered death upon the cross for me.

Enable me to praise and adore the blessed Spirit, Who sanctifies and illumines the mind; Who co-operates with the means of grace; Who condescends to visit and assist and refresh my soul by His powerful influences.

Glory be to the Father, Son, and Holy Spirit, joint Authors of my salvation! Amen.

God's Favor in Christ[22]

The noblest wine, the most generous cordial, does not so much exhilarate and cheer the Spirit as the least perception of your favor through Jesus Christ does refresh and gladden the soul.

And all the more, when the soul is ready to faint under the weight of its corrupt nature, and when we have been in an unsuccessful pursuit of happiness—in the enjoyment of what the world calls good.

It is in these lucid intervals, when the soul by contemplation holds You in view, that we say with Your Apostle: "Master, it is good for us to be here!"

Supreme Eternal Being! Fountain of life and happiness! Vouchsafe to be forever present to the inward sense of my mind; and as I offer You my heart take possession by Your Holy Spirit.

Loving God[23]

How hard I find it to be upon the guard, to maintain a constant watch, and a regular habitual advertence to my thought, words, and actions. And this

---

21   Doughty, ed., *Prayers of Susanna Wesley*, 31.

22   McMullen, ed., *Prayers and Meditations*, 81.

23   McMullen, ed., 31, retitled here by me.

irregularity of temper and life that interrupts the comforts which might be found in religion and renders my perseverance suspicious.

But this is my infirmity. I ought to consider that God is always the same, fixed, immutable, ever ready to succor and strengthen them that truly and sincerely devote themselves to His service.

The whole tenor of the Gospel insists upon sincerity as the main condition of salvation. A sincere faith and obedience, though the one may be weak and the other imperfect, yet if they do but determine a person to an habitual temper of obedience; if they do but in the main prove a person devoted to God; and that though they cannot with St. Peter appeal to that Omniscient Being that they do love Him, yet if they can but heartily say: "Lord, You that know all things, know that I desire nothing more than to love You."[24]

Surely God will make great allowances for infirmities, temptations, sudden and unforeseen accidents, nor ought I so frequently to admit of nice scruples, and perplexing thoughts, but rather employ my thoughts and time in a strict, conscientious performance of present duty, and so entirely depend on the infinite goodness of God to secure me from future temptations. Glory be to You, O Lord! Amen.

Watch and Pray[25]

You have called us, O Lord, to watch and pray [Mt. 26:41]. Therefore, whatever may be the sin against which I pray, make me careful to watch against it, and so have reason to expect that my prayer will be answered.

In order to perform this duty aright, grant me; grace to preserve a sober, equal temper; sincerity to pray for Your assistance; remembering also that sobriety and equality of mind consist in freedom from all perturbation. Amen.

Commitment and Obedience[26]

Morning and evening I commit my soul to Jesus Christ, the Savior of the world. Enable me, O God, to observe what He says to me; resolutely to

---

24 This may be an allusion to John 21:17.

25 McMullen, ed., *Prayers and Meditations*, 37.

26 Doughty, ed., *Prayers of Susanna Wesley*, 39.

obey His precepts and endeavor to follow His example in those things wherein He is exhibited to us as a pattern for our imitation.

Make plain to me that no circumstance nor time of life can occur but I may find something either spoken by our Lord Himself or by His Spirit in the prophets or apostles that will direct my conduct, if I am but faithful to Thee and my own soul. Amen.

On Anxiety[27]

Be with me, O God, in a time of deep adversity, which is apt to affect my mind too much and to dispose to anxious, doubtful and unbelieving thoughts.

May I give way to no direct murmurings, no repinings at the prosperity of others, no harsh reflections on Providence, but may I maintain a constant acknowledgement of Thy justice and goodness.

Save me from thinking severely or unjustly of others; from being too much dejected or disposed to peevishness, covetousness, or negligence in affairs from working too much or too little. Forbid that I should ever wholly omit to implore Thy divine blessings and assistance in honest prospects and endeavors or be too solicitous and earnest in prayer for external blessings.

May no slight access of trouble have power to ruffle my temper, and to indispose or distract my mind in my addresses to heaven, in reading, meditation, or any other spiritual exercise. I would ever lay to heart the words of our Lord: "Be careful (anxious) for nothing. Therefore I say unto you, Be not anxious for the morrow."[28] Amen.

To Live Wholly a Christian[29]

I have found, O God, that the Christian religion is of so complicated a nature that I must give myself entirely to its discipline, if I would steadfastly adhere to any of its principles.

All virtues are closely bound together, and I find that in breaking but one like of the golden chain I spoil the whole contexture. So do

---

27　Doughty, ed., 40–41.

28　This is an allusion to Matthew 6:34, "Take therefore no thought for the morrow: for the morrow shall take thought for the things of itself."

29　Doughty, ed., *Prayers of Susanna Wesley*, 42.

virtues mutually strengthen and assist virtues: temperance and chastity; fortitude and truth; humility and patience; divine charity and charity toward man.

All virtues, of what denomination soever, reciprocally cherish and invigorate one another. Grant grace, O Lord, to be wholly a Christian. Amen.

Living the Gospel[30]

Lord, why do I not take more care to practice my own rules? For what reason or for what do I write them down if not that I might remember to practice them in my life in the world?

Help me, therefore, to keep my affections under control and to be careful not to offend in speaking of persons who are absent; for I am convinced that it is my duty so to do, not to be guilty this matter, lest by sinning against the checks of the conscience, I provoke the Holy Spirit to forsake me.

An Irreligious Mind[31]

Deliver me, O God, from a vain and irreligious mind, that, engrossed in the things of the world, fails to note the withdrawal of vital influences and becomes insensible to the grace and comfort of Thy Holy Spirit.

Enable me to love Thee above all things; to have a higher estimation of Thee than of any other and of all things that Thou hast created. May I be incapable of rest or satisfaction of mind under a sense of Thy displeasure! Help me to clear accounts with Thee, that I may then fully use the innocent enjoyments of life. Amen.

Guard My Words[32]

Enable me, O God, to keep a due regard over my words, that I may habitually speak nothing but what is true on all occasions. Show me what a high

---

30 McMullen, ed., *Prayers and Meditations*, 63.
31 Doughty, ed., *Prayers of Susanna Wesley*, 49.
32 Doughty, ed., 52.

offense it is against the God of Truth to speak falsely, either through design or inadvertence.

In telling any story or relating past actions may I be careful to speak deliberately and calmly, avoiding immoderate uncharitableness and excessive anger on the other, lest invention supply the defect of my memory.

May I ever remember that I am in the presence of the great and holy God, and that every sin is a contradiction and offense to some Divine attribute, and that lying is opposite and offensive to Thy truth. Amen.

Cultivating a Habitual Sense of God[33]

Almighty God, Whom my reason declares to be the Author of my being and from Whom derive all things necessary for my support, enable me to practice an unfeigned subjection of myself toward Thee.

Save me from the lack of consideration and advertence to these first principles of religion. May I be careful to maintain a constant, habitual sense of Thee in my mind; to live and act as in Thy presence; to think often of Thy power, wisdom, goodness, justice, truth, and above all, of Thine infinite purity, that it may be a check on my mind and the best preservative against all temptations. Amen.

True Friendship[34]

Enable me to live so as to deserve a friend, and if I never have one on earth, You be my friend, for in having You, I shall have all that is dear and valuable in friendship.

Though a good name is as precious in friendship, yet I remember that I have offered up mine to you, my God, and have resolved never to make my reputation or the esteem of man [to be] the end of my actions, where Your glory is not concerned. Amen.

---

33 Doughty, ed., *Prayers of Susanna Wesley*, 53, with slight modification of the language.

34 McMullen, ed., *Prayers and Meditations*, 3.

A Good Conscience[35]

Lord, I resolve to keep a conscience void of offense towards You and man, for I see how many nowadays seek to advance their worldly interest; endeavor to raise their families by fraud and oppression; and who make shipwreck of their faith and good conscience.

Let it, then, be my great care to have a special regard to justice and charity; to preserve the principles of faith inviolate, and in all cases to perform present duty with the greatest exactness and integrity.

For I know that whenever crosses or troubles are met without because of you, Lord, all will be well within. Amen.

Cleanse My Heart and Mind[36]

Great and holy God, I have much need of humbling myself before You, because of the sins that I am daily guilty of; in thought, word, and deed, against Your Divine Majesty.

Help me, Lord, to overcome habitual levity in my thoughts and to shun vain and impure thoughts which, though they do not take up their abode in my mind for any length of time, yet in their passing through often leave a tincture of impurity.

Enable me to watch over my heart, thoughts and affections with all diligence, for out of them are the issues of life. How often have I offended in this way! Cleanse me, Lord, from my secret faults, for out of the abundance of the heart the mouth speaks [Mt. 12:34].

Help me, my God, to guard against vain and unnecessary words, and to speak of You with that reverence, that humility, that gravity that I ought. Amen.

Family Responsibilities[37]

I know, Lord, that though the care and education of so many children must create abundance of trouble and will perpetually keep the mind

---

35 McMullen, ed., 18.
36 McMullen, ed., 43.
37 McMullen, ed., 20.

employed—as well as the body; yet I will consider it no small honor to be entrusted with the care of so many souls. For I know too, Lord, that if that trust be but managed with prudence and integrity, the harvest will abundantly recompense the toil of the seed-time.

Help me to know too, that it will be certainly no little accession to the future glory to stand forth at the last day and say, "Lord, here are the children which You have given me, of whom I have lost none by my ill example; nor by my neglecting to instill into their minds, in their early years, the principles of Your true religion and virtue." Amen.

A Prayer of Thanks[38]

My God and Father, though often interrupted by bodily infirmities, grant me patience and submission, remembering that obedience is better than sacrifice.[39]

I thank Thee for my being and preservation, my food and raiment, but chiefly for what is infinitely more than all we can receive of temporal blessings, in that Thou hast sent Thine only Son into the world to save sinners, and for this one infinite and inestimable mercy I would praise and adore Thee to all eternity. Amen.

Peace of Conscience[40]

I thank Thee, O God, for the peculiar joy that comes with peace of conscience and for the pleasure and satisfaction of soul when it is strengthened by Thy grace to perform the several duties of life.

Help me, in the extraordinary occurrences of life, to keep my mind from being too warm and from speaking too eagerly.

I trust Thee with all events and beg Thy blessing upon my honest endeavors. Do Thou help me to guard my mind this day and inspire me with devotion in singing Thy praise. Amen.

---

38 Doughty, ed., *Prayers of Susanna Wesley*, 55.
39 An allusion to 1 Samuel 15:22, "Behold, to obey is better than sacrifice."
40 Doughty, ed., *Prayers of Susanna Wesley*, 56.

For a Life of Holiness[41]

Almighty God, I cannot possibly aspire vigorously toward Thee or have any clear perception of spiritual things without the assistance of Thy grace. Only the same almighty power that raised Jesus Christ from the dead can raise this soul of mine from the death of sin to a life of holiness.

I do not question that power and I believe that these desires proceed from Thee. Give me faith and patience. Help me to wait for Thine enabling grace without discouragement, remembering the words of our Savior, that we ought always to pray and not faint [Lk. 18:1]. Amen.

Seize the Opportunity[42]

When I examine myself three times a day, help me to do it more accurately; let no trifling matter divert me, for though it takes not much time, it is certain that opportunities once lost can never be recovered.

May it be that whatever my hand finds to do, I will do with all my might. When I have an opportunity, therefore, I will thankfully and vigorously make use of it, remembering that for all these things God will bring me to judgment.

Savior, I remember that when on earth You went about doing good. I must also do what good I can, especially to the souls God has committed to my care and help me not to be discouraged by infirmities or work. Amen.

Cleanse Me, O Lord[43]

Cleanse me, O Lord, from my secret faults, and keep me from presumptuous sins, lest they get the dominion over me.

Remind me, Lord, when I would attempt the conversion of others that I must be careful in the first place to reform myself. And if I do not abstain myself from gross and scandalous vices I am of all others the most unfit for a reformer.

---

41 Doughty, ed., 57, with the language slightly modified.
42 McMullen, ed., *Prayers and Meditations*, 7.
43 McMullen, ed., 42.

God, the Great Lord of heaven and earth, the Almighty Father of Spirits, has placed all mankind in this world in a state of probation, and has committed to each individual a stock of talents, to some more, to some less, commanding us to improve them for His glory. Help me, therefore, to look upon every child as a talent committed to my trust.

And my I be assured that I must give an account at the last great day how I have discharged this trust, and if through my default any soul miscarry, how will I hold up my face in the last judgment? Amen.

Deliver Us from Temptation[44]

I resolve not to be discouraged in times of bodily weakness. All the more will I endeavor to keep my mind as composed as possible and I will pray to You, Lord, to preserve me from temptation during these times—and that as my day is long so my strength might be.

Though You as a merciful being never expose us or lead us into temptation with a design to ensnare or betray of virtue, yet oftentimes for reasons not always obvious, You do permit ill men and evil angels, to afflict Your servants very severely.

Help us to remember that in Jesus You tell us: happy is the man that endures temptation, with submission I would pray. Blessed is the man whom God by his Providence preserves from too great or constant trials. Amen, Lord Jesus.

Help Me to Know Myself[45]

O Lord, as defects and infirmities betray themselves in the daily accidents and common conservations of life, grant me Your grace, that I may watch over, regulate and govern them.

Enable me to know myself and those with whom I have to do, that I may conform to the precepts of the Gospel and train myself to those rules of wisdom and virtue of which I am capable.

Help me to discern the proper season and the just occasion of every virtue, and then to apply myself to attain it, by exercising it in those

---

44 McMullen, ed., 64.
45 McMullen, ed., 15.

beneficent activities which, for want of due reflection, may not seem of any great importance. Amen.

God Answers Prayer[46]

God is Truth, and it is obviously impossible that Your Word should ever fail. You never said to any of Your creatures; "Seek ye my face or favor" in vain. And again You said, "Ask and ye shall receive, seek and ye shall find, knock and it shall be opened unto you."

Why is it then that my prayers are not answered? It cannot be that You are unmindful or unwilling or unable to grant my petitions. Why then should it be? I am asking from myself and I receive not, because I ask amiss.

I either ask irreverently, which is rather a demanding than a begging grace, which argues lack of reverence and humility; or I ask coldly without being appraised of the value of that grace that I pray for, and so I do not in good earnest desire it. It is no wonder I see no answer.

Perhaps my desires spring, not from a principle of love to God and a high estimation of holiness, nor from a zeal for Your glory and a hearty desire to be conformed to Your image and will, but it may be I ask for grace that I may be assured of Your protection in this world.

Perhaps I aske that I may enjoy a greater affluence of temporal blessings, or that I may be applauded and esteemed by man; and can one really believe that will prostitute His noblest gifts to such an unworthy creature?

You are a great and jealous God, nor will You admit a rival in Your love; to such as would divide their affections between Him and the world. We must give You all our heart, or You will accept of none of it.

You require that such as take upon themselves the honor of speaking to You, should approach You with the most profound humility; with the highest reverence and devotion; with a heart separated from the world; devoted to Your glory; and that we most highly esteem, value and prize the grace which we petition for.

For what greater affront can we offer your Divine Majesty than to aske with seeming devotion any virtue or grace when we do not have the least regard whether we have it or not?

---

46 McMullen, ed., 28–30.

But suppose we offer our petitions to the Divine Majesty, with the utmost profound reverence; with humility; with an earnest desire of those things we pray for; and with an ardent zeal for the manifestations of His glory, yet perhaps we ask impatiently, we would indeed have grace, but we would have it just then, we are not willing to tarry the Lord's leisure.

Nor are we willing to be at the pains of repeating our petitions, and therefore we are delayed, though not denied, our mind, instead of being more strongly united to by faith and love, grows displeased and angry. We say, "What a weariness it is to serve the Lord? Or what profit is it that we serve the Almighty?"[47]

Whether these or any other reasons prevent the answering of prayers, this we may be assured of, that God is infinite truth, and since He has graciously promised to hear the prayers that are made to Him in the name of Christ, He will certainly do it. Amen.

Redeeming the Time[48]

Lord, I would begin and end the day with you—the Alpha and Omega—and in it I really experience what it is to love you; then I will redeem all the time I can for your immediate service.

For I remember the rule I lived under when in my father's house, when I had as little—if not less—liberty than I have now, I used to allow myself as much time for recreation as I spent in private devotion; not that I always spent so much, but I have myself leave to go so far but no farther.

A Morning Prayer[49]

It is too common with me upon receiving any light, or new supply of grace, to think, now I have gained my point, and may say, "Soul, take thine ease," by this means I think not of going any further, or else fall into dejection of spirit, upon a groundless fear that I shall soon lose what I have gained, and in a little time be never the better for it.

---

47 This question is based on Job 21:15.
48 McMullen, ed., *Prayers and Meditations*, 8.
49 Dr. John Whitehead, *The Life of Rev. John Wesley, M.A. . . . With Some Account of His Ancestors and Relations* (Boston: Jm. McLeish, 1844), 39.

Both these are sins. The first proceeds from immoderate love of present ease and spiritual sloth; the other from want of faith in the all-sufficiency of my Savior.

We must never take up our rest on this side of heaven, nor think we have enough of grace or enjoy enough of God till we are perfectly renewed and sanctified in body, soul, and spirit; till we are admitted into that blessed region of pure and happy spirits where we shall enjoy the beatific vision according to the measure of our capacities. Nor must we, out of a pretended humility, because we are unworthy of the least mercy, dare to dispute or question the sufficiency of the merits of Jesus Christ. It is impossible for God Incarnate to undertake more than He is able to perform. Amen.

A Prayer at Noon[50]

To know God only as a philosopher, to have the most sublime and curious speculations concerning His essence and attributes, His providence, to be able to demonstrate His being from all or any of the works of nature, and to discourse with the greatest elegancy and propriety of words of His existence or operations—will avail us nothing unless at the same time we know Him experimentally; unless the heart perceive and know Him to be its Supreme good and only happiness, unless the soul feel and acknowledge that she can find no repose, no peace, no joy, but in loving and being beloved by Him; and does accordingly rest in Him as the center of her being, the fountain of her pleasure, the origin of all virtue and goodness, her light, her life, her strength, her all; everything she wants or wishes in this world, and forever! In a word, HER LORD, [and] HER GOD!

Thus, let me ever know Thee, O God! I do not despise nor neglect the light of reason, nor that knowledge of Thee which by her conduct may be collected from the goodly system of created beings, but this speculative knowledge is not the knowledge I want and wish for."

---

50 Rev. Adam Clarke, *Memoirs of the Wesley Family* (New York: Lane and Tippett, 1848), 378.

An Evening Prayer[51]

I give Thee praise, O God, for a well-spent day. But I am yet unsatisfied, because I do not enjoy enough of Thee. I would have my soul more closely united to Thee by faith and love. I would love Thee above all things.

Thou, Who has made me, knowest my desire, my expectation. My joys all center in Thee and it is Thou Thyself that I desire; it is Thy favor, Thine acceptance, the communications of Thy grace that I earnestly wish for, more than anything in the world.

I rejoice in my relation to Thee, Who art my Father, my Lord, and my God. I rejoice that Thou hast power over me and that I desire to live in subjection to Thee. I thank Thee that Thou hast brought me so far. I will beware of despairing of Thy mercy for the time which is to come and will give Thee the glory of Thy free grace. Amen.

A Reflection at Noon[52]

What can human reason do, or how far can the light of reason direct us to find out the knowledge of the Most High? From the primordials of the universe we collect that there is One supreme, eternal, consequently self-existent, Being, Who gave being to all things; since to act presupposes existence, for nothing can act before it be.

That this Being must possess, by way of eminence, all the perfections we discern in the creatures, reason tell us, for nothing can impart that to another which it has not to impart.

An Evening Prayer[53]

If to esteem and to have the highest reverence for Thee! If constantly and sincerely to acknowledge Thee, the Supreme, the Only desirable Good, to love Thee, I do love Thee!

If comparatively to despise and undervalue all the world contains, which is esteemed great, fair or good; if earnestly all the world constantly

---

51 Doughty, ed., *Prayers of Susanna Wesley*, 46.

52 Clarke, *Memoirs of the Wesley Family*, 377.

53 Whitehead, *Life of Rev. John Wesley*, 40.

to desire Thee, Thy favor, Thy acceptance, Thyself, rather than any or all things Thou hast created, by to love Thee, I do love Thee!

If to rejoice in Thy essential majesty and glory! If to feel a vital joy o'erspread and cheer the heart at each perception of Thy blessedness, at every thought that Thou art God; that all things are in Thy power; that there is none superior or equal to Thee—be to love Thee, I do love Thee!

Before the Lord's Supper[54]

O Lord, that we might always prepare ourselves when we come to the Lord's Supper.

That we would examine ourselves whether we truly repent of our former sins; steadfastly purpose to lead new lives; have a lively faith in God's mercy through Christ, with a thankful remembrance of His death; and be in charity with all men.

---

54 McMullen, ed., *Prayers and Meditations*, 39, edited by the author.

Appendix C

Selected Prayers by John Wesley

Time for God[1]

Deliver me, O God, from too intense an application to even necessary business. I know how this dissipates my thoughts from the one end of all my business and impairs that lively perception I would ever retain of Thee standing at my right hand.

I know the narrowness of my heart, and that an eager attention to earthly things leaves it no room for the things of heaven. O teach me to go through all my employments with so truly disengaged a heart that I may still see Thee in all things, and see Thee therein as continually looking upon me, and searching my heart, and that I may never impair that liberty of spirit which is necessary for the love of Thee. Amen.

God's Hands[2]

Into Thy hands we commend both our souls and bodies which Thou hast mercifully preserved this day. We trust in Thy watchful providence who givest Thy angels charge over us, Who art about our beds, and about our paths, and spiest out all our thoughts.

---

1   Michael McMullen, ed., *Hearts Aflame: Prayers of Susanna, John and Charles Wesley* (London: Holy Trinity Church, 1995), 10.
2   McMullen, ed., 22.

Continue these holy thoughts and desires in us till we fall asleep, that we may receive the light of morning with a new joy in Thee and thankful affection to Thee. Amen.

Looking Forward[3]

Pardon, good Lord, all my former sins, and make me every day more zealous and diligent to improve every opportunity of building up my soul in Thy faith, love, and obedience. Make Thyself always present to my mind, and let Thy love fill and rule my soul in all those places, companies, and employments, to which Thou callest me this day.

In all my passage through this world, suffer not my heart to be set upon it, but always fix my single eye and my undivided affections on the prize of my high calling. This one thing let me do; let me so press towards this, as to make all things else minister unto it; and be careful so to use them, as thereby to fit my soul for that pure bliss which Thou hast prepared for those that love You. Amen.

The Watching Shepherd[4]

Thou Shepherd of Israel, vouchsafe to receive me this night and ever into Thy protection. Accept my poor services and pardon the sinfulness of these and all my holy duties. Let it be Thy good pleasure to put a period to sin and misery, to infirmity and death, and to hasten Thy Kingdom; that we, with all that wait for Thy salvation, may eternally love and praise Thee, O God the Father, God the Son and God the Holy Ghost, throughout all ages, world without end.

God Is All We Need[5]

Gracious Father, keep us, we pray Thee, this day in Thy fear and favor, and teach us in all our thoughts, words, and works, to live in Thy glory.

---

3   McMullen, ed., 13.
4   McMullen, ed., 19.
5   McMullen, ed., 26.

If Thou guide us not, we go astray; if Thou uphold us not, we fall. Let Thy good providence be our defense, and Thy good Spirit our Guide and Counsellor, and Supporter in all our ways.

And grant that we may do always what is acceptable in Thy sight, through Jesus Christ our Lord, in Whose holy Name we close these our imperfect prayers. Amen.

Prayer and Praise to the Trinity[6]

Glory be to Thee, O most adorable Father, Who after Thou hadst finished the work of creation, entered into Thy eternal rest.

Glory be to Thee, O holy Jesus, Who having through the eternal Spirit, offered Thyself a full, perfect, and sufficient sacrifice for the sins of the whole world, didst rise again the third day from the dead, and hadst all power given Thee both in heaven and on earth.

Glory be to Thee, O blessed Spirit, Who proceeding from the Father and the Son, didst come down in fiery tongues on the Apostles, on the first day of the week, and didst enable them to preach the glad tiding of salvation to a sinful world, and has ever since been moving on the faces of men's souls, as Thou didst once on the face of the great deep, bringing them out of that dark chaos in which they were involved.

Glory be to Thee, O holy undivided Trinity, for jointly concurring in the great work of our redemption and restoring us again to the glorious liberty of the sons [and daughters] of God.

Glory be to Thee, Who in compassion to human weakness, hast appointed a solemn day for the remembrance of Thy inestimable benefits. Amen.

In Praise of God's Creation[7]

Thou art praised, O Lord, by all Thy works, and magnified by everything which Thou hast made.

---

6   McMullen, ed., 36–37, modified somewhat.
7   McMullen, ed., 46.

The sun rejoiced to run his course, that he may set forth Thy praise Who madest him. Nor do the moon and stars refrain to manifest Thy glory, even amidst the silent night.

The earth breathes forth perfumes, as incense to Thee, her sacred King. Who hast crowned her with herbs and trees and beautified her with hill and dales.

The deep uttereth her voice, and lifteth up her hands on high to Thee, the great Creator, the universal King, the everlasting God.

Thy floods clap their hands, and the hills are joyful together before Thee. Thy fruitful vales rejoice and sing Thy praise.

The Example of Christ[8]

May the example of our blessed Savior be always dear to us, that we may cheerfully follow Him in every holy temper and delight to do Thy will, O God.

Let these desires which Thou hast given us never die or languish in our hearts but be kept always alive in their vigor and force by the perpetual inspirations of the Holy Ghost. Amen.

Following Jesus Christ[9]

O Thou Who didst cast seven devils out of Mary Magdalene, cast out of my heart all corrupt affections.

O Thou Who didst cleanse the lepers, heal the sick, and give sight to the blind, heal the diseases of my soul, open my eyes and fix them singly on the prize of my high calling, and cleanse my heart from every desire but that of advancing Thy glory.

O Jesus, poor and abject, unknown and despised, have mercy upon me and let me not be ashamed to follow Thee.

O Jesus, hated, calumniated, and persecuted, have mercy upon me and let me not be afraid to come after Thee.

---

8   Donald E. Demaray, comp., *Devotions and Prayers of John Wesley* (Grand Rapids, MI: Baker Book House, 1957), 97.

9   Frederick C. Gill, ed., *The Prayers of John Wesley* (Nashville: Abingdon-Cokesbury, 1951), 48–50, shortened slightly.

O Jesus, betrayed and sold at a vile price, have mercy upon me and make me content to be as my Master.

O Jesus, blasphemed, accursed, and wrongfully condemned, have mercy upon me and teach me to endure the contradiction of sinners.

O Jesus, clothed with a habit of reproach and shame, have mercy upon me and let me not seek my own glory.

O Jesus, insulted, mocked and spit upon, have mercy upon me and let me run with patience the race set before me.

O Jesus, dragged to the pillar, scourged, and bathed in blood, have mercy upon me and let me not faint in the fiery trial.

O Jesus, crowned with thorns and hailed in derision;

O Jesus, burdened with our sins and the curses of the people;

O Jesus, affronted, outraged, buffeted, overwhelmed with injuries, griefs, and humiliations;

O Jesus, hanging on the accursed tree, bowing the head, giving up the ghost, have mercy upon me and conform my whole soul to Thy holy, humble, suffering Spirit.

O Thou who for the love of me hast undergone such an infinity of sufferings and humiliation, let me be wholly emptied of myself, that I may rejoice to take up my cross and daily follow Thee.

Meekness and Humility[10]

O Lamb of God, Who both by Thy example and precept didst instruct us to be meek and humble; give me grace throughout my whole life in every thought, word, and work to imitate Thy meekness and humility. Mortify in me the whole body of pride. Amen.

Father of Mercies[11]

May all my thoughts, words, and works tend to thy glory. Heal, O Father of mercies, all my infirmities; strengthen me against all my follies; and forgive me all my sins and let them not cry louder in Thine ears for vengeance than my prayers [cry out] for mercy and forgiveness.

---

10 Demaray, comp., *Devotions and Prayers*, 105.

11 McMullen, ed., *Hearts Aflame*, 54.

Lord Have Mercy[12]

O God the Father, Who canst not be thought to have made me only to destroy me, have mercy upon me.

O God the Son, Who knowing Thy Father's will, didst come into the world to save me, have mercy upon me.

O God, the Holy Ghost, Who to the same end hast so often breathed holy thoughts into me, have mercy upon me.

O Holy, Blessed and Glorious Trinity, Whom in Three Persons, I adore as One God, have mercy upon me.

Building Up My Soul[13]

Pardon, good Lord, all my former sins, and make me every day more zealous and diligent to improve every opportunity of building up my soul in Thy faith, love, and obedience.

Make Thyself always present to my mind, and let Thy love fill and rule my soul in all those places, companies and employments to which Thou callest me. Amen.

The Great Love of God[14]

Most gracious Lord, Who hast so loved the world that Thou gavest Thyself to redeem it, and humbly tookest upon Thee our nature that Thou mightest suffer as man for the sins of men for our salvation; do Thou fill our souls with a sense of Thy wonderful love, that we may live in Thy goodness, die in Thy favor, and rise again to rejoice with Thee forever in Thy glory. Amen.

To Be Filled with God[15]

When we have received any favor from God, we might to retire, if not into our closets, into our hearts, and say, "I come, Lord, to restore to You

---

12 McMullen, ed., 57.

13 Demaray, comp., *Devotions and Prayers,* 57, from Wesley's *Collection of Prayers.*

14 Demaray, comp., 99.

15 McMullen, ed., *Hearts Aflame,* 61, from Wesley's *Christian Perfection.*

what You have given, and I freely relinquish it, to enter again into my own nothingness."

For what is the most perfect creature in heaven or earth in Your presence, but a void capable of being filled with You and by You, as the air which is void and dark is capable of being filled with the light of the sun, who withdraws it every day to restore it the next, there being nothing to the air that either appropriates this life or resists it.

O give me the same faculty of receiving and restoring Your grace and good works! I say Yours, for I acknowledge the root from which they spring is You, and not in me.

Rule My Heart Without Rival[16]

I confess it is by duty, to love Thee my God, with all my heart. Give Thy strength unto Thy servant, that, Thy love may fill my heart, and be the motive of all the use I make of my understanding, my affections, my sense, my health, my time, and whatever other talents I have received from Thee.

Let This, O God, rule my heart without a rival, let it dispose all my thoughts, words, and works, thus only can I fulfil my duty and thy command, of loving Thee with all my heart, and mind, and soul, and strength.

God's Fatherly Protection[17]

O my God, I praise Thee for Thy continual preservation of me, for Thy fatherly protection over me this day, for all the comforts with which Thou hast surrounded me, spiritual and temporal, particularly for leave now to pray unto Thee.

Accept my poor services; pardon the sinfulness of this and all my holy duties; and bless me, my friends, and relations, my benefactors and mine enemies, this night, and forever, with the blessings of Thy children. Amen.

---

16 McMullen, ed., 66, from *Wesley's Collection of Prayers.*
17 McMullen, ed., 103, from *Wesley's Collection of Prayers.*

Wholly unto God[18]

Grant, O Lord, that I may look for nothing, and resent nothing; that I may go through all the scenes of life, not seeking my own glory, but looking wholly unto Thee and acting wholly for Thee. Amen.

Life as Prayer[19]

God's command to pray without ceasing is founded on the necessity we have of His grace, to preserve the life of God in the soul, which can no more subsist one moment without it than the body can [do] without air.

Whether we think of or speak to God, whether we act or suffer for Him, all is prayer, when we have no other object [in view] than His love, and the desire of pleasing Him.

All that a Christian does, even in eating and sleeping is prayer, when it is done in simplicity; according to the order of God, without either adding to or diminishing from it by His own choice.

Perfect Prayer[20]

Prayer continues in the desire of the heart, tho' the understanding be employed on outward things. In souls filled with love, the desire to please god is a continual prayer.

As the furious hate which the devil bears us is termed the roaring of the lion, so our vehement love may be termed crying after God.

God only requires of His adult children that their hearts be truly purified, and that they offer Him continually the wishes and vows that naturally spring from perfect love.

For these desires, being the genuine fruits of love, are the most perfect prayers that can spring from it.

---

18 Demaray, comp., *Devotions and Prayers*, 101.
19 McMullen, ed., *Hearts Aflame*, 82. From Wesley's *Christian Perfection*.
20 McMullen, ed., 83. From Wesley's *Christian Perfection*.

A Prayer on Stewardship[21]

Teach us, O God, to use this world without abusing it; and to receive the things needful for the body, without losing our part in Thy love which is better than life itself. Amen.

Useful in the World[22]

Make us faithful in all our contacts with our neighbors, that we may be ready to do good and bear evil, that we may be just and kind, merciful and meek, peaceable and patient, sober and temperate, humble and self-denying, inoffensive and useful in the world; that so glorifying Thee here we may be glorified with Thee in Thy heavenly kingdom. Amen.

God's Mighty Love[23]

May there ever abide in us such a strong and powerful sense of Thy mighty love toward us in Christ Jesus as may constrain us freely and willingly to please Thee in the constant exercise of righteousness and mercy, temperance and charity, meekness and patience, truth, and fidelity, together with such a humble, content and peaceable spirit as may adorn the religion of our Lord and Master. Amen.

Governed by God's Will[24]

We offer up our souls and bodies to Thee, to be governed, not by our own will, but Thine. Let it ever be the joy of our hearts to be under the conduct of Thine unerring wisdom, to follow Thy counsels and to be ruled in all things by Thy will. And let us never distrust Thy abundant kindness and tender care over us. Amen.

---

21 Demaray, comp., *Prayers and Devotions*, 19.
22 Demaray, comp., 107.
23 Demaray, comp., 31.
24 Demaray, comp., 35.

Strength and Love[25]

Give me Thy strength; give me Thy love; and be the motive of all the use I make of my understanding, my affections, my senses, my health, my time, and whatever other talents I have received from Thee.

Thus only can I fulfill my duty and Thy command of loving Thee with all my heart, and mind and soul and strength. Amen.

A Divided Heart[26]

Is there a thing beneath the sun
That strives with Thee my heart to share?
Ah, tear it thence, and reign alone.
The Lord of every motions there!
Then shall my heart from earth be free,
When it hath found repose in Thee. Amen.

Love Towards Neighbor[27]

Let Thy unwearied and tender love to me make my love unwearied and tender to my neighbor, zealous to pray for and to procure and promote his health and safety, ease and happiness. Make me peaceable and reconcilable, easy to forgive, and glad to return good for evil. Amen.

Hearing God's Voice[28]

Each moment draw from earth away
My heart, that lowly waits Thy call;
Speak to my inmost soul, and say,
"I am Thy Love, Thy God, Thy All!"
To feel Thy power, to hear Thy voice,
To taste Thy love, be all my choice. Amen.

---

25 Demaray, comp., 23.
26 Demaray, comp., 37.
27 Demaray, comp., 27.
28 Demaray, comp., 45.

Devoted to God's Service[29]

My Father, I am Thy humble servant, whom Thou hast preserved, who lives by Thy power this day.

I bless and glorify Thee for Thine almighty providence, and humbly pray Thee that this and all my days may be wholly devoted to Thy service. Amen.

My Joy[30]

Still, let Thy wisdom be my guide,
Nor take Thy flight from me away;
Still with me let Thy grace abide,
That I from Thee may never stray:
Let Thy Word richly in me dwell,
Thy peace and love my portion be;
My joy to endure and do Thy will,
Till perfect I am found in Thee. Amen.

Full Possession of My Heart[31]

Take Thou the full possession of my heart, raise there Thy throne, and command there as Thou dost in heaven.

Being created for Thee, let me ever act for Thy glory. Being redeemed by Thee, let me render unto Thee what is Thine, and let my spirit ever cleave to Thee alone. Amen.

Giving Oneself to God[32]

I give Thee my understanding: may it be my only care to know Thee, Thy perfections, Thy works, and Thy will.

---

29 Demaray, comp., 51.
30 Demaray, comp., 75.
31 Demaray, comp., 73.
32 McMullen, ed., *Hearts Aflame*, 85–87, from John Wesley's *Collection of Prayers*.

I give Thee my will. May I have no will of my own. Whatsoever Thou willest may I will and that only. May I will Thy glory in all things as Thou doest and make that my end in everything.

I give Thee my affections. Do Thou dispose of them all. Be Thou my love, my fear, my joy. And may nothing have any share in them but with respect to Thee and for Thy sake.

What Thou lovest may I love; what Thou hatest may I hate; and that in such measure as Thou are pleased to prescribe me.

I give Thee my body. May I glorify Thee with it and preserve it holy, fit for Thee, O God, to dwell in. May I neither indulge it nor use too much rigor toward it, but keep it, as far as in me lies, healthy, vigorous, and active, and fit to do Thee in all manner of service, which Thou shalt call for.

I give Thee all my worldly goods. May I prize them and use them only for Thee. May I faithfully restore to Thee, in Thy poor, all Thou has entrusted me with, above the necessities of my life, and be content to part with them too, whenever Thou, my Lord, shalt require them at my hands.

I give Thee my credit and reputation. May I never value them but only in respect of Thee; nor endeavor to maintain them but as they may do Thee service and advance Thy honor in the world.

I give Thee myself and my all. Let me look upon myself to be nothing and to have nothing, out of Thee. Be Thou the sole disposer and governor of myself and all I have. Be Thou my portion and my all.

O my God and my all, when hereafter I shall be tempted to break this solemn engagement, when I shall be pressed to conform to the world, and to the company and customs that surround me, may my answer be: I am not my own. I am not for myself, nor for the world, but for my God. I will give unto God the things which are God's. God be merciful to me a sinner. Amen.

Constant Devotion[33]

O God, purify my heart that I may entirely love thee and rejoice in being loved of Thee; that I may confide in Thee, and absolutely resign myself to Thee, and be filled with constant devotion toward Thee; that I may never sink into a base love of anything below nor be oppressed with the cares of

---

33 Demaray, comp., *Prayers and Devotions*, 77.

this life; but assist me to abhor that which is evil and cleave to that which is good. Amen.

Christ In Me[34]

O Hide this self from me that I
No more, but Christ in me, may live;
My vile affections crucify,
Nor let one darling lust survive!
In all things nothing may I see,
Nothing desire or seek, but Thee. Amen.

A New Creature[35]

O Savior of the world, Thou that hast destroyed the power of the devil, that hast overcome death, That sitteth at the right hand of the Father, Thou that will speedily come down in Thy Father's glory to judge all men according to their works; be Thou my Light and my Peace. Destroy the power of the devil in me and make me a new creature. Amen.

For Our Family[36]

O that all the habitations of Christians may be the house of prayer! Let Thy blessing rest upon us of this family. In every condition secure our hearts to Thyself and make us ever to approve ourselves sincere and faithful in Thy service. Amen.

For Those with Various Concerns[37]

Give Thy grace, O holy Jesus, to all the world, and let all who are redeemed by Thy blood acknowledge Thee to be the Lord. Let all Christians, especially those of this nation, keep themselves unspotted from the world.

---

34 Demaray, comp., 15.
35 Demaray, comp., 79.
36 McMullen, ed., *Hearts Aflame*, 105, from Wesley's *Collection of Prayers*.
37 McMullen, ed., 110, retitled. From Wesley's *Collection of Prayers*.

Be a help at hand to all that are afflicted and assist them to trust in Thee. Raise up friends for the widow and fatherless, the friendless, and oppressed.

Give patience to all that are sick, comfort to all troubled consciences, strength to all that are tempted. Amen.

Never Weary of Doing Us Good[38]

Thou are never weary, O Lord, of doing us good. Let us never be weary of doing Thee service. Let us take pleasure in Thy service and abound in Thy work and in Thy love and praise evermore.

Fill up all that is lacking, reform whatever is amiss in us, perfect the thing that concerns us, and let the witness of Thy pardoning love ever abide in all our hearts. Amen.

The Sense of God's Acceptance[39]

Search us, O Lord, and prove us. Look well if there be any wickedness in us and lead us in the way everlasting.

Let Thy favor be better to us than life itself, that so in all things we may approve our hearts before Thee and feel the sense of Thy acceptance of us, giving us a joy which the world cannot give. Amen.

Daily Renewed[40]

O Lord, the God of our salvation, Thou still watchest over us for good; Thou daily renewest to us our lives and Thy mercies; and Thou hast given us the assurance of Thy Word that if we commit our affairs to Thee, Thou wilt direct our paths. Amen.

---

38 Demaray, comp., *Devotions and Prayers,* 67; Wesley's "wanting" has been modernized to "lacking."

39 Demaray, comp., 71.

40 Demaray, comp., 53.

God Who Strengthens and Supports[41]

Strengthen all Thy faithful servants. Bring back them that wander out of the way. Raise up those that are fallen. Confirm those that stand, and grant them steadily to persevere in faith, love and obedience. Relieve and comfort all that are in distress.

Let the earth bring forth her fruit in due season and let all honest and industrious people be blest in their labors. Remember all those who have done good unto us. Grant forgiveness and charity to all our enemies and continue goodwill among all our neighbors.

Support the sick with faith and patience. Assist those who are leaving this world. Receive the souls which Thou hast redeemed with Thy Son's precious blood, and sanctified by the Holy Spirit, and give us all a glorious resurrection and eternal life.

The Whole Armor of God[42]

Thou knowest, O Lord, all our temptations. Thou knowest the devices of the enemy and the deceitfulness of our own hearts.

We pray Thee, good Lord, that Thou wilt arm us with the whole armor of God. Uphold us with Thy free Spirit and watch over us for good evermore. Amen.

Our Map and Guide[43]

O Lord, bow down Thy gracious eye and pity the frailties of our imperfect nature.

Reach forth Thy hand and strengthen us with Thy grace, that nothing may divert our advance toward Thee.

In this dangerous labyrinth of the world and the whole course of our pilgrimage here, let Thy heavenly dictates be our map and Thy holy life be our guide. Amen.

---

41 McMullen, ed., *Hearts Aflame*, 115. From Wesley's *Collection of Prayers*, retitled here.
42 Demaray, comp., *Devotions and Prayers*, 59. See also Charles Wesley's hymn, "The Whole Armor of God," in Appendix D.
43 Demaray, comp., 55.

Guide of My Ways[44]

Send Thy Holy Spirit to be the Guide of all my ways and the sanctifier of my soul and body. Save, defend, and build me up in Thy fear and love. Give unto me the light of Thy countenance, peace from heaven, and the salvation of my soul in the day of the Lord Jesus. Amen.

The Ship of Our Bodies[45]

O God, Whose eternal providence has embarked our souls in the ship of our bodies, prevent us from anchoring in any sea of this world, but help us to steer directly through it to Thy glorious kingdom; preserve us from the dangers that on all sides assault us, and keep our affections still fitly disposed to receive Thy holy inspirations, that being carried strongly forward by Thy Holy Spirit we may happily arrive at last in the haven of eternal salvation, through our Lord Jesus Christ. Amen.

For Pardon and Peace[46]

In Christ's name we come to beg Thy pardon and peace, the increase of Thy grace and tokens of Thy love; for we are not worthy of the least of Thy mercies.

But worthy is the Lamb that was slain to take away the sin of the world, for whose sake Thou wilt give us all things. Amen.

Our Whole Duty[47]

Let Thy mighty power enable us to do our duty toward Thee and toward all men with care, diligence, zeal, and perseverance.

Help us to be meek and gentile in our conversation, prudent and discreet in ordering our affairs, observant of Thy fatherly providence in

---

44 Demaray, comp., 65.
45 Demaray, comp., 63.
46 Demaray, comp., 61.
47 Demaray, comp., 95.

everything that befalls us, thankful for Thy benefits, patient under Thy chastisements, and readily disposed for every good word and work. Amen.

For the Brethren[48]

Let no temptation expose me to ingratitude or make me forfeit Thy loving-kindness which is better than life itself. But grant that I may assist all my brethren with my prayers where I cannot reach them with actual services. Make me zealous to embrace all occasions that may minister to their happiness. Let Thy love to me be the pattern of my love to them.

Whole-Hearted Service[49]

We implore Thy tender mercies in the forgiveness of all our sins and we desire to devote our whole person, body, soul, and spirit to Thee. As thou dost inspire us with these desires, so accompany them always with Thy grace, that we may every day with our whole hearts give ourselves up to Thy service. Amen.

Bearing Us Up[50]

We depend upon Thee, especially for the grace of Thy Holy Spirit. May we feel it perpetually bearing us up, by the strength of our faith, above the temptations that may at any time assault us. Amen.

Glorifying God[51]

O God, fill my soul with so entire a love of Thee that I may love nothing but for Thy sake. Give me grace to study Thy knowledge daily, that the more I know Thee, the more I may love thee. Let it be the one business of my

---

48 McMullen, ed., *Hearts Aflame*, 95, from Wesley's *Collection of Prayers*.
49 Demaray, comp., *Devotions and Prayers*, 85. Wesley's "whole man" has been altered to "whole person."
50 Demaray, comp., 93.
51 Demaray, comp., 91.

life to glorify Thee, by every word of my tongue and by every work of my hand. Amen.

For the Church[52]

Bless, O gracious Father, all the nations whom Thou hast placed upon the earth, with the knowledge of Thee, the only true God; but especially bless Thy holy catholic church and fill it with truth and grace.

Where it is corrupt, purge it; where it is in error, rectify it; where it is right, confirm it; where it is divided and rent asunder, heal the breaches thereof.

Replenish all who Thou hast called to any office therein, with truth of doctrine and innocency of life. Let their prayers be as precious incense in Thy sight, that their cries and tears for the City of God may not be in vain. Amen.

God's Holy Spirit and the Church[53]

O God, who by Thy Holy Spirit didst at first establish a church, and Who, sanctifying it by the same Spirit, still preserve and govern it; hear, we beseech Thee, and mercifully grant us the perpetual assistance of Thy grace.

That we may never be deceived by any false spirit, nor overcome by the suggestions of flesh and blood, but in all our doubts may be directed in the ways of truth, and in all our actions, guided by this Thy Holy Spirit. Who, with Thee, and Thy eternal Son, liveth and reigneth, one God, world without end. Amen.

A Prayer of Thanksgiving:[54]

I humbly and heartily thank Thee for all the favors Thou hast bestowed on me; for creating me after Thine own image, for daily preserving me by Thy good providence.

---

52 McMullen, ed., *Hearts Aflame*, 112, retitled here.
53 McMullen, ed., 115, retitled here.
54 Demaray, comp., *Devotions and Prayers*, 13.

I also thank Thee for Thy temporal blessings; for the preservation of me, for my health, strength, food, raiment, and all the other comforts and necessities of life. Amen.

A Prayer of Thanksgiving[55]

O most great and glorious God, Who art mighty in Thy power and wonderful in Thy doings toward the sons of men; accept, I beseech Thee, my unfeigned thanks and praise for my creation, preservation, and all the other blessings which in the riches of Thy mercy Thou hast from time to time poured down upon me. Amen.

In Everything Give Thanks[56]

Lift our affections to things above, that we may have perfect contentment in well-doing and patient suffering.

Free us from the cares of this world, from all distrust of Thy good providence, from repining at anything that befalls us; and enable us in everything to give thanks, believing that all things are ordered wisely and shall work together for good. Amen.

Daily Devoted[57]

Accept, O Lord, my gratitude for all the benefits Thou hast given me, for the good things of this life and the hope of eternal happiness. To Thy holy name be ascribed the honor and glory.

Oh, let the sense of all Thy blessings have this effect upon me—to make me daily more diligent in devoting myself, all I am, and all I have to thy glory. Amen.

---

55 Demaray, comp., 41.
56 Demaray, comp., 109.
57 Demaray, comp., 83.

Beginning the Day Right[58]

O that we could begin this day in devout meditations, in joy unspeakable, and in blessing and praising Thee, Who hast given us such good hope and everlasting consolation.

Lift up our minds above all these little things below, which are apt to distract our thoughts; and keep them above till our hearts are fully bent to seek Thee every day, in the way wherein Jesus that gone before us. Amen.

A Prayer for Sunday Morning[59]

Search us, O Lord, and prove us; try out our reins and heart. Look well if there be any way of wickedness in us and lead us in the way everlasting. Let Thy favor be better to us than life itself; that so in all things we may approve our hearts before Thee, and feel the sense of Thy acceptance of us, giving us joy which the world cannot give.

And accept, good Lord, of all the praises of all Thy people met together this day. O that "thy ways were known upon all the earth, Thy saving health among all nations;" and that all Christian rulers, especially, may be willed with Thy Holy Spirit, and be faithful subjects of the Lord Jesus, "the King of kings, and Lord of lords."

O that Thy "priests may be clothed with righteousness, and Thy saints rejoice and sing;" that all who are in distress may trust in Thee, the "health of their countenance, and their God." O Lord, bear us, and make Thy face to shine upon Thy servants, that we may "enter into Thy gates with thanksgiving, and into Thy courts with praise; that we may be thankful unto Thee and bless Thy name."

Amen, for Jesus Christ's sake; in whose words we conclude our imperfect prayers, saying: "Our Father."

---

58 McMullen, ed., *Hearts Aflame*, 25.

59 Thomas Jackson, ed., *The Works of John Wesley, A.M.*, 14 vol. (London: Wesleyan Conference, 1872), Vol. XI, 238–39, with omissions and modernization of some words.

A Prayer for Sunday Evening[60]

Blessed be Thy goodness for that great consolation, and for the assistance of Thy Holy Spirit. Bless be Thy goodness, that we have felt it so often in our hearts, inspiring us with holy thoughts, filling us with love and joy, and comfortable expectations of "the glory that shall be revealed." We thank Thee, that Thou hast allowed us this day to attend on Thee in public service; and that we have begun, in any measure, to pursue after that eternal "rest which remaineth for the people of God."

We offer up again our souls and bodies to Thee to be governed, not by our will, but Thine. O let it be ever the ease and joy of our hearts, to be under the conduct of Thy unerring wisdom, to follow Thy counsels, and to be rule in all things by Thy holy will. And let us never distrust Thy abundant kindness and tender care over us; whatsoever it is Thou wouldst have us to do or to suffer in this world.

O God, purify our hearts, that we may entirely love Thee, and rejoice in being beloved of Thee; that we may confide in Thee, and absolutely resign ourselves to Thee, and be filled with constant devotion toward Thee.

O that we may never sink into a base love of anything here below, nor be oppressed with the cares of this life; but assist us to "abhor that which is evil, and cleave to that which is good,' Let us use this world as not abusing it." Give us true humility of spirit that we may "not think of ourselves more highly than we ought to think." Keep us from being "wise in our own conceits." "Let our moderation be known to all men." Make us "kindly affectioned one to another;" to delight in doing good; to "show all meekness to all men"; to "render to all their dues; tribute to whom tribute is due, custom to whom custom, fear to whom fear, honor to whom honour"; and to "owe no man anything, but to love one another."

Make us happy with them that we may be able to "love our enemies"; to bless those that curse us, to do good to them that hate us; to rejoice with them that do rejoice, and weep with them that weep. Compose our spirits to a quiet and steady dependence on Thy good providence, that we may "take no thought for our life," nor "be careful for anything, but by

---

60 Jackson, ed., Wesley's "Prayers for Families," 239–40, with omissions and modernization of some words.

prayer and supplication with thanksgiving, still make known our requests to Thee our God."

And help us "to pray always and not faint; in every thing to give thanks, and offer up the sacrifices of praise continually; to rejoice in hope of Thy glory"; to "possess our souls in patience"; and to "learn in whatsoever state we are therewith to be content." Make us, "know both how to be abased, and how to abound; everywhere, and in all things," instruct us "both to abound and to suffer want," being enabled to "do all things through Christ which strengtheneth us." Amen.

A Prayer for the Morning[61]

We humble ourselves, O Lord of heaven and earth, before Thy glorious Majesty. We acknowledge Thy eternal power, wisdom, goodness, and truth; and desire to render Thee most unfeigned thanks, for all the benefits which Thou pourest upon us; but above all, for Thine inestimable love, in the redemption of the world by our Lord Jesus Christ.

We implore Thy tender mercies in the forgiveness of all our sins, whereby we have offended either in thought, word, or deed. We desire to be truly sorry for all our misdoings, and utterly to renounce whatsoever is contrary to Thy will. We desire to devote our whole person, body, soul, and spirit, to Thee. And as Thou doest inspire us with these desires, so accompany them always with Thy grace, that we may every day, with our whole hearts, give ourselves up to Thy service.

We desire to be so holy and undefiled as our blessed Master was. And we trust Thou wilt fulfill all the gracious promises which He hath made to us. Let them be dearer to us than thousands of gold and silver; let them be the comfort and joy of our hearts. We ask nothing, but that it may be unto Thy servants according to His word.

Thou has mercifully kept us the last night; blessed be Thy continued goodness. Receive us likewise into Thy protection this day. Guide and assist us in all our thoughts, words, and actions. Make us willing to do and suffer what Thou pleases; waiting for the mercy of our Lord, Christ Jesus, unto eternal life. Amen.

---

61 Jackson, ed., 241. This is John's Prayer "For Monday Morning." The original phraseology has been modernized slightly.

A Prayer for the Evening[62]

Almighty and most merciful Father, in Whom we live, move, and have our being; to Whose tender compassion we owe our safety the day past, together with all the comforts of this life, and the hopes of that which is to come; we praise Thee, O Lord, we bow ourselves before Thee, acknowledging we have nothing but what we receive from Thee. "Unto Thee do we give thanks [Ps. 75:1]," O God, Who daily pourest Thy benefits upon us.

Blessed be Thy goodness for our health, for our food and raiment, for our peace and safety, for the love of our friends, for all our blessings in this life, and our desire to attain that in our hearts any motion toward Thee. Behold, O Lord, we present ourselves before Thee, to be inspired with such a vigorous sense of Thy love, as may put us forward with a greater earnestness, zeal, and diligence in all our duty. Renew in us, we beseech [Thee], a lively image of Thee, in all righteousness, purity, mercy, faithfulness, and truth. O that Jesus, the hope of glory, may be formed in us, in all humility, meekness, patience, and an absolute surrender of our souls and bodies to Thy holy will; that we may not live, but Christ may live in us; that every one of us may say, "The Life I now live in the flesh, I live by faith in the Son of God, Who loved me, and gave Himself for me [Gal. 2:20]."

Let the remembrance of His love, Who made Himself an offering for our sins, be ever dear and precious to us. Let it continually move us to offer up ourselves to Thee, to do Thy will, as our blessed Master did. May we place an entire confidence in Thee, and still trust ourselves with Thee, Who has not "spared Thine own Son, but freely given Him up for us all" [Rom. 8:32]. May we humbly accept of whatsoever Thou sendest us, and "in everything give thanks [1 Thes. 5:18]." Surely Thou "wilt never leave us nor forsake us [1 Kings 8:57]." O Guide us safe through all the changes of this life, in an unchangeable love to Thee, and a lively sense of Thy love to us, till we come to live with Thee and enjoy Thee forever.

And now that we are going to lay ourselves down to sleep, take us into Thy gracious protection, and settle our spirits in such quiet and delightful thoughts of the glory where our Lord Jesus lives, that we may desire to . . .

---

62 Jackson, ed., 242–43; From Wesley's "Prayers for Families"; this prayer was "For Monday Evening."

go to Him who died for us, that, whether we wake or sleep, we might live together with Him. Amen.

A Prayer for the Morning[63]

O most great and mighty Lord, the Possessor of heaven and earth, all the angels rejoice in blessing and praising Thee, the Father of spirits; for "Thou hast created all things, and in wisdom hast Thou made them all [Ps. 104:24]," and spread Thy tender mercies over all thy works. We desire thankfully to acknowledge Thy bounty to us, among the rest of Thy creatures, and Thy particular grace and favor to us in Jesus Christ, our merciful Redeemer. O give us a deep sense of that love which gave Him to die for us, that He might be "the Author of eternal salvation to all them that obey Him [Heb. 5:9]."

And hast Thou not said, that Thou wilt "give Thy Holy Spirit unto them that ask it?" [1 Thes. 4:8]? O Father of mercies, let it be unto us according to Thy word. Cherish whatever Thou hast already given us, which is acceptable in Thy sight. And since at the best we are unprofitable servants and can do no more than it is our duty to do, enable us to do everything which Thou hast commanded us heartily, with good-will, and true love to Thy service.

O that we might ever approach Thee with delight and feel it the joy of our hearts to think of Thee, to praise Thee, to give Thee thanks, and to offer ourselves with absolute resignation to Thee. O that mercy may always please us, as it pleaseth Thee; that we may be strictly just and righteous; may cheerfully pass by injuries, freely deny ourselves whatever is not for Thy glory; willingly submit to Thy fatherly corrections and perform the duties of our several relations with singleness of heart. Render us so mindful of the great love of our Lord, that we may be zealously concerned for His glory, and use our utmost diligence to promote His religion in the world; delighting to commemorate His death and passion, making a joyful sacrifice of our souls and bodies to Him, and earnestly desiring that His Kingdom may come over all the earth. . . .

---

63   Jackson, ed., 244–45, from Wesley's "Prayers for Families"; this is his prayer "For Tuesday Morning" with a few slight alterations in phraseology and some omissions.

And O that all people may be awakened into a lively and thankful sense of all Thy benefits. Stir up especially the minds of all Christian people to follow "the truth as it is in Jesu [Eph. 4:21]," and exercise themselves "to have a conscience void of offence towards God and towards man [Acts 4:16]." . . . O that true religion, justice, mercy, brotherly kindness, and all things else that are praiseworthy, may so flourish among us, that we may enjoy the blessings of peace and plenty, and there may be no complaining in our streets.

We recommend to Thee all our friends, and neighbors, all the poor, the sick, and the afflicted, desiring those mercies for them which we would ask for ourselves, were we in their condition. "O God, whose never-failing providence ordereth all things in heaven and earth, keep them and us, we beseech Thee, from all hurtful things, and give us those things which are profitable for us, according to Thine abundant mercy in Lord Jesus." Amen.

Grace Before Meals[64]

O Lord, I beseech Thee, give Thy blessing with what Thy mercy has here provided me with, that whether I eat or drink, or whatsoever I do, I may do all to Thy glory and praise, through Jesus Christ my Lord. Amen.

Grace After Meals[65]

O Lord my God, bless Thy Holy Name for this mercy, which I have now received from Thy bounty and goodness. Feed now my soul with Thy grace, that I may make it my meat and drink to do Thy gracious will, through Jesus Christ my Savior. Amen.

---

64 McMullen, ed., 27.
65 McMullen, ed., 28.

Appendix D

Charles Wesley's Hymns as Preludes to Prayer

Before Private Prayer[1]

Father of Jesus Christ, my Lord,
I humbly seek Thy face,
Encouraged by the Savior's word
To ask Thy pardoning grace.

Entering into thy closet,[2] I
The busy world exclude,
In secret prayer for mercy cry;
And groan to be renewed.

Thy grace I languish to receive,
The Spirit of love and power,
Blameless before Thy face to live,
To live and sin no more.

Fain would I all Thy goodness feel,
And know my sins forgiven,

1   William Osborn, *The Poetical Works of John and Charles Wesley*, 13 vols. (London: Methodist Conference, 1872), Vol. IV, #39, 259–60.
2   Cf. Matthew 6:6, "When thou prayest, enter into thy closet, and when thou hast shut thy door, pray to thy Father which is in secret."

And do on earth Thy perfect will,
As angels do in heaven.

O Father, glorify Thy Son,
And grant what I require,
For Jesu's sake the Gift send prove,
And answer me by fire.

Kindle the flame of love within
Which may to heaven ascend,
And now the word of grace begin,
Which shall in glory end.

For Believers Praying[3]

Come, ye followers of the Lord,
In Jesu's service join;
Jesus gives the sacred word,
The ordinance divine;
Let us His command obey,
And ask, and have, whate'er we want:
Pray we, every moment pray,
And never, never faint.

For Believers Praying[4]

The praying Spirit breathe,
The watching power impart,
From all entanglements beneath
Call off my peaceful heart;
My feeble mind sustain,
By worldly thoughts oppressed;

---

3   Franz Hildebrandt and Oliver Beckerlegge, eds., *The Works of John Wesley Vol. VII, A Collection of Hymns for the Use of the People Called Methodists* (Nashville: Abingdon, 1983), #286, 438, the first verse of four, based on Luke 18:1.

4   Hildebrandt and Beckerlegge, eds., #287, 439–40.

Appear and bid me turn again
To my eternal rest.

Swift to my rescue come,
Thy own this moment seize,
Gather my wand'ring spirit home
And keep in perfect peace;
Suffer no more to rove
O'er all the earth abroad,
Arrest the prisoner of Thy love,
And shut me up in God.

For Believers Praying[5]

Lord, that I may learn of Thee,
Give me true simplicity;
Wean my soul, and keep it low,
Willing Thee alone to know.

Let me cast my reeds aside,
All that feeds my knowledge pride,
Not to man, but God submit,
Lay my reasonings at Thy feet.

Then infuse the teaching grace,
Spirit of truth and righteousness;
Knowledge, love divine impart,
Life eternal to my heart.

A Prayer for the Light of Life[6]

O Sun of Righteousness, arise,
With healing in Thy wing!

---

5   Hildebrandt and Beckerlegge, eds., #293, (verses 1, 2, and 4), 446–57. Capitalization altered.
6   Osborn, ed., *Poetical Works*, Vol. II, 12.

To my disease, my fainting soul
Life and salvation bring.

These clouds of pride and sin dispel
By Thy all-piercing beam;
Lighten mine eyes with faith, my heart
With holy hope inflame.

My mind by Thy all-quickening power
From low desires set free;
Unite my scatter'd thoughts, and fix
My love entire on Thee.

Father, Thy long-lost son receive;
Savior, Thy purchase own;
Blest Comforter, with peace and joy
Thy new-made creature crown!

Eternal, undivided Lord,
Co-equal One and Three!
On Thee all faith, all hope be placed,
All love be paid to Thee!

A Prayer For Faith[7]

Father, I stretch my hands to Thee,
No other help I know:
If Thou withdraw Thyself from me,
Ah! Whither shall I go?

What did Thy only Son endure
Before I drew my breath!
What pain, what labor to secure
My soul from endless death

O Jesu, could I this believe,
I now should feel Thy power;

---

7   Osborn, ed., Vol. II, 13–14.

Now my poor soul Thou wouldst retrieve,
Nor let me wait one hour.

Author of faith, to Thee I lift
My weary, longing eyes;
O, let me now receive that gift;
My soul without it dies.

Surely Thou canst not let me die!
O, speak, and I shall live!
And here I will unwearied lie,
Till Thou Thy Spirit give.

The worst of sinner would rejoice,
Could they but see Thy face:
O, let me hear Thy quickening voice,
And taste Thy pardoning grace!

Praying for a Blessing[8]

Spirit of faith, come down,
Reveal the things of God,
And make to us the Godhead known,
And witness with the blood:
Tis Thine the blood to apply,
And give us eyes to see,
Who did for every sinner die
Hath surely died for me.

No man can truly say
That Jesus is the Lord
Unless Thou take the veil away;
And breathe the living word;
Then, only then we feel
Our interest in His blood,
And cry with joy unspeakable,
Thou art my Lord, my God!

---

8   Hildebrandt and Beckerlegge, eds., *A Collection of Hymns*, #83, 182–83.

O that the world might know
The all-atoning Lamb!
Spirit of faith, descend, and show
The virtue of His name;
The grace which all may find,
The saving power impart,
And testify to all mankind,
And speak in every heart!

Inspire the living faith
(Which whoso'er receives,
The witness in himself he hath,
And consciously believes)
The faith that conquers all,
And doth the mountain move,
And saves who'er on Jesus call,
And perfects them in love.

For Believer's Watching[9]

Jesu, my Savior, Brother, Friend,
On Whom I cast my every care,
On Whom for all the things I depend,
Inspire, and then accept my prayer.
If I have tasted of Thy grace,
The grace that sure salvation brings,
If with me now Thy Spirit stays,
And hovering hides me in His wings.

Still let Him with my weakness stay,
Nor for a moment's space depart,
Evil and danger turn away,
And keep, till He renews my heart.

When to the right or left I stray,
His voice behind me may I hear;

---

9   Hildebrandt and Beckerlegge, eds., #303, 458–59, capitalization altered.

"Return and walk in Christ thy way;
Fly back to Christ; for sin is near."

His sacred unction from above,
Be still my comforter and guide,
Till all the stony He remove,
And in my loving heart reside.

Jesus, I fain would walk in Thee,
From nature's every path retreat;
Thou art my way, my leader be,
And set upon the rock my feet.

Uphold me, Savior, or I fall;
O reach me out thy gracious hand!
Only on Thee for help I call;
Only by faith in Thee I stand.

Before Reading the Scriptures[10]

Come Holy Ghost, our hearts inspire,
Let us Thine influence prove,
Source of the old prophet's fire
Fountain of life and love.

Come, Holy Ghost (for moved by Thee
The prophets wrote and spoke);
Unlock the truth, Thyself the key,
Unseal the sacred book.

Expand Thy wings, celestial dove,
Brood o'er our nature's night;
On our disordered spirits move,
And let there now be light.

God through himself we then shall know,
If Thou within us shine,

---

10 Hildebrandt and Beckerlegge, eds., #85, 185.

And sound, with all Thy saints below,
The depths of love divine.

Before Reading the Scriptures[11]

Inspirer of the ancient seers,
Who wrote from Thee the sacred page,
The same through all succeeding years;
To us in our degenerate age
The Spirit of Thy Word impart
And breathe the life into our heart.

While now Thine oracles we read
With earnest prayer and strong desire,
O let Thy Spirit from Thee proceed
Our souls to waken and inspire,
Our weakness help, our darkness chase,
And guide us by the light of grace.

Whene'er in error's paths we rove,
The living God through sin forsake,
Our conscience by Thy Word reprove,
Convince, and bring the wanderers back;
Deep wounded by Thy Spirit's sword,
And then by Gilead's balm restored.

The secret lessons of Thy grace
Transmitted through the Word, repeat,
And train us up in all Thy ways
To make us in Thy will complete;
Fulfil Thy love's redeeming plan,
And bring us to a perfect man.

Furnished out of Thy treasury,
O may we always ready stand
To help the souls redeemed by Thee
In what their various states demand;

---

11   Hildebrandt and Beckerlegge, eds., #87, 186–87, capitalization altered.

To reach, convince, correct, reprove,
And build them up in holiest love.

The Whole Armor of God[12]

Soldiers of Christ, arise
And put your armor on,
Strong in the strength which God supplies
Through His eternal Son;
Strong in the Lord of hosts,
And in His mighty power,
Who in the strength of Jesus trust
Is more than conqueror.

Stand then in His great might,
With all His strength endued,
But take, to arm you for the fight,
The panoply of God;
That having all things done
And all your conflicts passed,
Ye may o'ercome through Christ alone,
And stand entire at last.

Stand then against your foes
In close and firm array;
Legions of wily fiends oppose
Throughout the evil day;
But meet the sons of night,
But mock their vain design,
Armed in the arms of heavenly light,
Of righteousness divine.

Leave no unguarded place,
No weakness of the soul;
Take every virtue, every grace,
And fortify the whole;

---

12 Hildebrandt and Beckerlegge, eds., #258, 399–400, capitalization altered.

Indissolubly joined,
To battle all proceed,
But arm yourselves with all the mind
That was in Christ your head.

Before the Lord's Supper[13]

Come, to the supper come,
Sinner, there still is room;
Every soul may be His guest,
Jesus give the general word;
Share the monumental feast,
Eat the supper of your Lord.

In this authentic sign
Behold the stamp Divine;
Christ revives His sufferings here,
Still exposes them to view;
See the Crucified appear,
Now believe He died for you.

The Lord's Supper as a Means of Grace[14]

Author of our salvation, Thee
With lowly thankful hearts we praise,
Author of this great mystery,
Figure and means of saving grace.

The sacred, true, effectual sign,
Thy body and Thy blood it shows;
The glorious instrument Divine
Thy mercy and Thy strength bestows.

We see the blood that seals our peace,
Thy pardoning mercy we receive;

---

13 Osborn, ed., *Poetical Works*, Vol. III, 211, "Hymns on the Lord's Supper," #8, 221.
14 Osborn, ed., *Poetical Works*, III, 236, "Hymns on the Lord's Supper, #28.

The bread doth visibly express
The strength through which our spirits live.

Our spirits drink a fresh supply,
And eat the bread so freely given,
Till borne on eagle's wings we fly,
And banquet with our Lord in heaven.

After the Sacrament[15]

How happy are Thy servants, Lord,
Who thus remember Thee?
What tongue can tell our sweet accord,
Our perfect harmony?

Who Thy mysterious supper share,
Here at Thy table fed,
Many, and yet but one we are,
One undivided bread.

One with the living Bread Divine
Which now by faith we eat,
Our hearts, and minds and spirits join,
And all in Jesus meet.

---

15 Osborn, ed., #65, 338–39, the first three of the original four verses.

Charles Wesley's Hymns as Prayers for Various Occasions

At Waking[1]

Giver and Guardian of my sleep,
To praise Thy name I wake:
Still Lord, Thy helpless servant keep,
For Thy own mercy's sake.

The blessing of another day
I thankfully receive;
O may I only Thee obey,
And to Thy glory live.

Vouchsafe to keep my soul from sin;
Its cruel power suspend,
Till all this strife and war within
In perfect peace shall end.

O respite me from self and pride,
Curb and keep down my will.
My appetite and passions chide,
And bid the sea to be still.

---

1   William Osborn, ed., *The Poetical Works of John and Charles Wesley*, 13 vols. (London: Methodist Conference,1872), Vol. II, 140, the first six verses of the original fourteen.

Upon me lay Thy mighty hand,
My words and thoughts restrain,
Bow my whole soul to Thy command,
Nor let my faith be vain.

Prisoner of hope, I wait the hour
Which shall salvation bring;
When all I am shall own Thy power
And call my Jesus King.

A Morning Hymn[2]

We lift our hearts to Thee,
O Day-star from on high!
The sun itself is but Thy shade,
Yet cheers both earth and sky.

O, let Thy orient beams
The night of sin dispense;
The mists of error and of vice
Which shade the universe!

How beauteous nature now!
How dark and sad before!
With joy we view the pleasing change,
And nature's God adore.

O, may no gloomy crime
Pollute the rising day!
Or Jesu's blood, like evening dew
Wash all the stains away.

May we this life improve,
To mourn for errors past,
And live this short-revolving day
As if it were our last.

---

2   Osborn, ed., 20–21.

To God the Father, Son,
And Spirit, One and Three,
Be glory, as it was, is now;
And shall for ever be.

Before . . . Going to Work[3]

Let us go forth, 'tis God commands;
Let us make haste away,
Offer to Christ our hearts and hands,
We work for Christ today.

When He vouchsafes our hands to use,
It makes the labor sweet;
If any now to work refuse
Let not the sluggard eat.

Who would not do what God ordains,
And promises to bless?
Who would not 'scape the toil and pains
Of sinful idleness?

In vain to Christ the slothful pray:
We have not learn'd Him so;
No; for He calls Himself the Way
And work'd Himself below.

Then let us in His footstep tread,
And gladly act our part;
On earth employ our hands and head,
But give Him all our heart.

In the Hurry of Business[4]

Help, Lord! the busy foe
Is as a flood come in!

---

3   Osborn, ed., 17–18.
4   Osborn, ed., *Poetical Works*, Vol. IV, #65, 54–55.

Lift up a standard and o'erthrow
This soul distracting sin;
Stem by that blood tree,
Nor let the rising torrent bear
My soul away from Thee.

The praying spirit breathe,
The watching power impart,
From all entanglements beneath
Call off my anxious heart:
My feeble mind sustain
By worldly thoughts oppress'd
Appear, and bid me turn again
To my eternal rest.

Swift to my rescue come,
Thine own this moment seize,
Gather my wandering spirit home,
And keep in perfect peace,
Suffer'd no more to rove
O'er all the earth abroad,
Arrest the prisoner of Thy love,
And shut me up in God.

For Believers Working[5]

Forth in Thy name, O Lord, I go,
My daily labor to pursue,
Thee, only Thee, resolved to know
In all I think, or speak, or do.

The task Thy wisdom has assigned
O let me cheerfully fulfil,
In all my works Thy presence find,

---

5   Franz Hildebrandt and Oliver Beckerlegge, eds., *The Works of John Wesley Vol. VII, A Collection of Hymns for the Use of the People Called Methodists* (Nashville: Abingdon, 1983), #315, 470, capitalization and spelling altered.

And prove Thy acceptable will.

Thee may I set at my right hand
Whose eyes my inmost substance see,
And labor on at Thy command,
And offer all my works to Thee.

Give me to bear Thy easy yoke,
And every moment watch and pray,
And still to things eternal look,
And hasten to Thy glorious day;

For Thee delightfully employ
Whate'er Thy bounteous grace hath given,
And run my course with even joy,
And closely walk with Thee to heaven.

For Believers Working[6]

Lo! I come with joy to do
The Master's blessed will,
Him in outward works pursue,
And serve His pleasure still.
Faithful to my Lord's commands,
I still would choose the better part,
Serve with careful Marth's hands,
And loving Mary's heart.

Careful, without care, I am,
Nor feel my happy toil,
Kept in peace by Jesu's name,
Supported by His smile;
I find His service my reward;
Every work do below
I do it to the Lord.

---

6   Hildebrandt and Beckerlegge, eds., #316. Verses 1 and 2 of 5, 470–71, capitalization
    altered.

Praying for Repentance[7]

Father of lights, from Whom proceeds
Whate'er Thy every creature needs,
Whose goodness, providentially nigh,
Feeds the young ravens when they cry;
To Thee I look; my heart prepare,
Suggest and hearken to my prayer.

Sure by Thy light myself I see
Naked, and poor, and void of Thee,
Thy eyes most all my thoughts survey,
Preventing what my lips would say;
Thou seest my wants, for help they call,
And ere I speak Thou know'st them all.

Fain would I know as known by Thee,
And feel indigence I see;
Fain would I all my vileness own,
And deep beneath the burden groan,
Abhor the pride that lurks within,
Detest and loathe myself and sin.

Ah, give me, Lord, myself to feel,
My total misery reveal;
Ah, give me, Lord (I still would say),
A heart to mourn, a heart to pray;
My business this, my only care,
My life, my every breath be prayer!

An Evening Hymn[8]

All praise to Him who dwells in bliss;
Who made both day and night;

---

7   Hildebrandt and Beckerlegge, eds., #96, 201–2, verses 1, 2, 4, 5.
8   Osborn, ed., *Poetical Works*, Vol. II, 27–28.

Whose throne is darkness, in the abyss
Of uncreated light.

Each thought and deed His piercing eyes
With strictest search survey;
The deepest shades no more disguise
Than the full blaze of day.

Whom Thou dost guard, O King of kings,
No evil shall molest;
Under the shadow of Thy wings
Shall they securely rest.

Thy angels shall around their beds
The constant stations keep;
Thy faith and truth shall shield their heads,
For Thou dost never sleep.

May we with calm and sweet repose,
And heavenly thoughts refresh'd
Our eyelids with the morn's unclose,
And bless the Ever-bless'd.

On Desiring to Love [Another][9]

O Love, I languish at Thy stay,
I pine for Thee with lingering smart.
Weary and faint through long delay:
When wilt Thou come into my heart?
From sin and sorrow set me free,
And swallow up my soul in Thee!

Come, O Thou universal Good!
Balm of the wounded conscience, come!
The hungry, dying spirit's food,
The weary, wandering pilgrim's home,

---

9   Osborn, ed., 13–14.

Haven to take the ship wreck'd in,
My everlasting rest from sin.

Be Thou, O Love, whate'er I want;
Support my feebleness of mind,
Relieve the thirsty soul, the faint
Revive, illuminate the blind,
The mournful cheer, the drooping lead,
And heal the sick and raise the dead!

Come, O my comfort and delight,
My strength and health, my shield and sun,
My boast, and confidence, and might,
My joy, my glory, and my crown,
My gospel-hope, my calling's prize,
My tree of life, my paradise.

The secret of the Lord Thou art,
The mystery so long unknown,
Christ in a pure and perfect heart,
The name inscribed in white stone,
The Life Divine, the little heaven,
My precious pearl, my present heaven.

A Prayer for Restoring Grace[10]

Jesus, Friend of sinners, hear,
Yet once again I pray;
From my debt of sin set clear,
For I have nought to pay:
Speak, O, speak the kind release,
A poor, backsliding soul restore;
Love me freely, seal my peace,
And bid me sin no more.

For my selfishness and pride,
Thou hast withdrawn Thy grace;

---

10   Osborn, ed., 119–20.

Let me long to wander wide,
An outcast from Thy face;
But I now my sins confess,
And mercy, mercy I implore:
Love me freely, seal my peace,
And bid me sin no more.

Though my sins as mountains rise,
And swell and reach to heaven,
Mercy is above the skies,
I may be still forgiven:
Infinite my sins' increase,
But greater is Thy mercy's store;
Love me freely, seal my peace,
And bid me sin no more.

Sin's deceitfulness hath spread
And hardness o'er my heart;
But if Thou Thy Spirit shed,
The stony shall depart;
Shed Thy love, Thy tenderness,
And let me feel the softening power;
Love me freely, seal my peace,
And bid me sin no more.

From the oppressive power of sin
My struggling spirit free:
Perfect righteousness bring in,
Unspotted purity;
Speak, and all this war shall cease,
And sin shall give its raging o'er:
Love me freely, seal my peace,
And bid me sin no more.

For this only thing I pray,
And this will I require,
Take the power of sin away;
Fill me with chaste desire;
Perfect me in holiness;

Thine image to my soul restore;
Love me freely, seal my peace,
And bid me sin no more.

A Prayer for Those Joined in Fellowship[11]

Jesu, united by Thy grace,
And each to each endear'd,
With confidence we seek Thy face,
And know our prayer is heard.

Still let us own our common Lord,
And bear Thine easy yoke—
A band of love, a threefold cord
Which never can be broke.

Make us into one spirit drink,
Baptize into Thy Name,
And let us always kindly think,
And sweetly speak the same.

Touch'd by the loadstone of Thy love,
Let all our hearts agree,
And ever towards each other move,
And ever move towards Thee.

To Thee inseparably join'd,
Let all our spirits cleave;
O may we all the loving mind
That was in Thee receive.

This is the bound of perfectness,
Thy spotless charity;
O let us (still we pray) possess
The mind that was in Thee.

---

11 Osborn, ed., 138–39. This is pt. IV, the first six of the original nine verses.

A Thanksgiving[12]

O what shall I do, my Savior to praise,
So faithful and true, so plenteous in grace;
So strong to deliver, so good to redeem
The weakest believer that hangs upon Him.

How happy the man whose heart is set free;
The people that can be joyful in Thee!
Their joy is to walk in the light of Thy face,
And still they are talking of Jesus's grace.

Their daily delight shall be in Thy name,
They shall as their sight Thy righteousness claim;
Thy righteousness wearing and cleansed by Thy blood,
Bold shall they appear in the presence of God.

For Thou art their boast, their glory and power;
And I also trust to see the glad hour,
My soul's new creation, a life from the dead,
The day of salvation, that lifts up my head.

For Jesus my Lord is now my defense,
I trust in His word, none plucks me from thence:
Since I have found favor He all things will do,
My King and my Savior shall make me anew.

Yea, Lord, I shall see the bliss of Thine own,
Thy secret to me shall soon be made known,
For sorrow and sadness I joy shall receive,
And share in the gladness of all that believe.

A Prayer for Laborers [Mt. 9:37][13]

LORD of the harvest, hear
Thy needy servants cry;

---

12 Osborn, ed., 176–77. Capitalization of the original has been altered.
13 Osborn, ed., 342–43.

Answer our faith's effectual prayer,
And all our wants ["lacks"] supply.

On Thee we humbly wait,
Our wants are in Thy view;
The harvest truly, Lord, is great,
The laborers are few.

Convert and send forth more
Into Thy church abroad,
And let them speak Thy word of power,
As workers with their God.

Give the pure gospel word,
The word of general grace;
Thee let them preach, the common Lord,
Savior of human race.

O let them spread Thy name,
Their mission fully prove,
The universal grace proclaim,
Thy all-redeeming love.

On all mankind forgiven
Empower them still to call,
And tell each creature under heaven
That Thou hast died for all.

At the Meeting of Friends[14]

All praise to our redeeming Lord,
Who joins us by His grace,
And bids us, each to each restored,
Together seek His face.

He bids us build each other up,
And gather'd into one

---

14 Osborn, ed., *Poetical Works*, Vol. IV, #32, 252–53.

To our high calling's glorious hope
We hand in hand go on.

The gift which He on one bestows,
We all delight to prove,
The grace through every vessel flows
In purest streams of love.
Even now we speak, and think the same,
And cordially agree,
Concentrated all through Jesu's name
In perfect harmony.

We all partake the joy of one,
The common peace we feel,
A peace to sensual minds unknown,
A joy unspeakable.
And if our fellowship below
In Jesus be so sweet,
What height of rapture shall we know
When round His throne we meet!

At the Parting of Friends[15]

Lord, we Thy will obey,
And in Thy pleasure rest,
We, only we, can say
Whatever is, is best,
Joyful to meet, and glad to part,
Assured we still are one in heart.

Hereby we sweetly know
Our love proceeds from Thee,
We let each other go,
From every creature free,
And cry, in answer to Thy call,
Thou art, O Christ, our all in all!

---

15   Osborn, ed., *Poetical Works*, Vol. V, 428–29.

Our Husband, Brother, Friend,
Our Counsellor Divine,
Thy chosen ones depend
On no support by Thine;
Our everlasting Comforter,
We cannot want, if Thou are here.

Still let us, gracious Lord,
Sit loose to all below,
And to Thy love restored
No other comfort know.
Stand fast in glorious liberty,
And live and die wrapp'd up in Thee.

For Believers Suffering[16]

Thee, Jesus, full of truth and grace
Thee, Savior, we adore;
Thee in affliction's furnace praise,
And magnify Thy power.

Thy power in human weakness shown
Shall glory in our Guide,
We now Thy guardian presence own,
And walk unburnt in fire.

Thee, Son of man, by faith we see,
And glory in our Guide,
Surrounded and upheld by Thee,
The fiery test abide.

The fire our graces shall refine
Till, molded from above;
We bear the character divine,
The stamp of perfect love.

---

16 Hildebrandt and Beckerlegge, eds., *Collection of Hymns*, #321, 486. The spelling
and capitalization have been altered.

Groaning for Redemption[17]

Come, Holy Ghost, all-quickening fire,
Come, and in me delight to rest!
Drawn by the lure of strong desire,
O Come, and consecrate by breast;
The temple of my soul prepare,
And fix Thy sacred presence there!

My peace, my life, my comfort Thou,
My treasure and my will all Thou art!
True witness of my sonship now
Engraving pardon on my heart,Seal of my sins in Christ forgiven,
Earnest of love, and pledge of heaven.

For the Mind of Christ[18]

Plant, and root, and fix in me
All the mind that was in Thee,
Settled peace I then shall find—
Jesu's is a quiet mind.

Anger I no more shall feel,
Always even, always still;
Meekly on my God reclined—
Jesu's is a gentle mind.

I shall suffer, and fulfil
All my Father's gracious will,
He in all alike resigned—
Jesu's is a patient mind.

When 'tis deeply rooted here
Perfect love shall cast out fear;

---

17 Hildebrand and Beckerlegge, eds., #363, Verses 1 and 3 of the original six, 532–33. Spelling and capitalization have been modernized.

18 Hildebrandt and Beckerlegge, ed., #345, 507–9, based on Phil. 2:3, "have the mind of Christ," verses 5–13 of the original.

Fear doth servile spirits bind—
Jesu's is a noble mind.

When I feel it fixed within
I shall have no power to sin;
How shall sin an entrance find?
Jesu's is a spotless mind.

I shall nothing know beside
Jesus, and Him crucified,
I shall all to Him be joined—
Jesu's is a loving mind.

I shall triumph evermore,
Gratefully my God adore,
God so good, so true, so kind—
Jesu's is a thankful mind.

Lowly, loving, meek, and pure,
I shall to the end endure;
Be no more to sin inclined
Jesu's is a constant mind.

I shall fully be restored
To the image of my Lord,
Witnessing to all mankind
Jesu's is a perfect mind.

CPSIA information can be obtained
at www.ICGtesting.com
Printed in the USA
FFHW020724231019
55733621-61594FF